THE ECONOMY IS...

THE GOVERNMENT IS...

CRIME AND PUNISHMENT IS...

THE MEDIA IS...

THE HEALTH CARE SYSTEM IS...

IMMIGRATION IS...

MESSED

UP!!!

DATING,MARRIAGE AND DIVORCE IS...

FOREIGN POLICIES ARE...

ORGANIZED RELIGION IS...

DISCRIMINATION AND RACISM ARE...

AMERICAN COMPANIES ARE...

MESSED UP!
What's Happening to Us, America?
Are We Fed Up Yet?

Todd M. Thiede

iUniverse, Inc.
New York Bloomington

Messed Up!
What's Happening to Us, America?
Are We Fed Up Yet?

iUniverse books may be ordered through booksellers or by contacting:

iUniverse
1663 Liberty Drive
Bloomington, IN 47403
www.iuniverse.com
1-800-Authors (1-800-288-4677)

Because of the dynamic nature of the Internet, any Web addresses or links contained in this book may have changed since publication and may no longer be valid.

ISBN: 978-1-4401-3170-7 (pbk)
ISBN: 978-1-4401-3171-4 (ebk)

Printed in the United States of America

iUniverse rev. date: 3/20/2009

DEDICATION

I wish to dedicate this book to:

My kids, who have to put up with all of my goofiness and all of my weird stories! I love you guys and would do anything for you!!

Tracy, the woman that listened to me rant and rave about all that I have put into this book. She is the one that told me I should write this book.

John, for allowing me to bounce all my wacky beliefs and stories off of him, and for our heated discussions about the said stories.

Mike Stefanik, thank you for the great drawings at the beginning of each chapter.

Merrill, thank you for reading this book and helping correct my many typo's and mistakes.

And last, but certainly not least, I want to dedicate this book to Kellie, who during my writing of this book gave me words of encouragement and support.

INTRODUCTION

I am not an author!! I am not a scholar!! I am also not a Republican or a Democrat. I am an American citizen that believes in common sense and reality. I believe that America is the best country in this whole world. I am a person who is saying what is on my mind, and I am sure it is on some of your minds as well. I firmly believe that I am speaking not just for me, but for the majority of the people in this country too.

With that being said, I also believe that things are not as they should be. Things have gone way off course in America. In 1776, our government was designed for the people, by the people. However, today our government is run by the government, for the rich and well off. (More about the government later in this book.)

I am writing this book as a person that is sick and tired of what is going on in this country; whether it is behind our backs or right in front of our faces. I am sick of being lied to, and sick of what I am seeing happen to our wonderful country by people that are out for only themselves. Most

Americans I truly believe think like I do, but do not act or can not act upon their feelings.

The one thing I can say about this is that we have lost focus of what is important in this country....THE PEOPLE!!!

I have said it before and I will say it again....this is really

MESSED UP!!!

WARNING!!!!!!

I want to take a minute to warn you about a few things before you start reading this book.

First, I tend to write like I talk. My writing style is a conversational one and sometimes I use colorful language from time to time. My intention here is not to be shocking or offensive, but simply to use real language, used by real people, in the real world.

When talking about government and real world problems it is hard not to be a LITTLE bit colorful.

If you are easily offended by colorful language and straight-talk this may not be the best book for you to read.

Second, I share a good deal of stories about real life experiences I've had with the world. Some of them from when I was hopeless and finding my way and some of them are from when I've become more experienced. Some of them are embarrassing and some of them are funny – but regardless, they all taught me valuable lessons and hopefully they'll teach you some lessons as well.

None of the stories in this book are made up. All of them are true. But the names have been changed or even left out to protect the privacy of the individuals. The important thing to note is not the details of the stories shared here, but the lessons behind them.

If you can get past my inexperienced writing style, you might actually learn a thing or two. You may even learn something that you can use to make this country and your life better.

Now on to the rest of the book...

Contents

DEDICATION vii

INTRODUCTION ix

WARNING!!!!!! xi

THE ECONOMY 1

AMERICAN COMPANIES. 37

OUR GOVERNMENT 51

FOREIGN POLICIES 71

THE MEDIA 91

DISCRIMINATION AND RACISM 111

IMMIGRATION 125

HEALTH CARE SYSTEM. 147

CRIME AND PUNISHMENT 165

DATING/MARRIAGE/DIVORCE 185

ORGANIZED RELIGION 225

CONCLUSION. 243

THE ECONOMY

The United States economy is sinking fast. Our government keeps trying to bail it out with different programs. First it was TARP and its 700 billion dollars. Now there is an economic stimulus package called TALF and its almost 800 billion dollars. Both of these plans are here because of the fact that our economy keeps getting worse and worse as time goes on. The Dow Jones Industrial Average has fallen to near 7000 in the early part of the year 2009. The Dow Jones Industrial Average is computed from the stock prices of 30 of the largest and most widely held public companies in the United States. Many people speculate it is going to get worse before it gets better. This chapter of my book is going to focus on some things that are wrong with our economy and how to fix it now. Yes, I mean now!! Not after it gets worse, but before it gets worse. I will also explain what has been done so far to help this economy (but it didn't actually help) and what can truly be done to fix our economy.

Here we are, the year is 2009, we have just had Barack Obama inaugurated as the 44th president of the United States. He promises change and an economic recovery. However, in my belief, this can't happen for many reasons. The housing market is one of the biggest of these reasons.

I have seen estimates projecting that there will be anywhere between 3 and 7 million homes foreclosed on in the year 2009. What will that do to the housing market? Every time a house is foreclosed on, it brings down other home values in that neighborhood, that town, and even that state. The reason this happens is because banks just want to sell the home for whatever they can get out of it just to recoup some of the money, rather than none of the money. That is their philosophy.

In 2008 the US government passed the TARP (Troubled Assets Relief Program) bill. This legislation is giving out 700 billion dollars to banks and insurance companies hoping that this influx of capital will give the banks confidence to lend again. The government is hoping that the banks will use it to trickle down to the American people and help the economy. What does trickle down to the American people mean you might be asking? It means that they are giving these billions of dollars to the bank to shore up their assets and the government in turn wants to have the banks give that money back to the people so they spend more and in turn help the economy. This has not been happening at all. I have a solution that would cost less than 1/3 of that 700 billion and the whole country would benefit, not just the banks and their executives.

We were all sold on the idea that part of the 700 billion TARP bill would be used to buy up troubled assets like mortgage securities that are defaulting and thus helping out the American people in dire straights. This has not been the case. Mr. Paulson (the man in charge of distributing the money as he sees fit) has announced that none of the money would be used for that after all. Excuse me? Wasn't that the main principle that the American people were told was going to happen with this money? Instead the money is given to major banks and insurance companies (AIG insurance in particular) for capital to lend out to get out of the mess we are in. In the TARP plan there are no rules as to how this money is to be used. What are the banks doing with this money? Well, I did read an article where they were spending hundreds of thousands of these dollars on perks (parties, vacations, etc) for the executives in the corporation and hoarding it to the point where they won't lend it out for fear of not getting it back. What does that do for our economy?NOTHING!!!!!!!!! So, instead of the money trickling to the people who need it, it stays in the rich persons hands (the people that don't need it the most) until this all blows over. I have news for them, it won't blow over until the middle and lower class receive their bailout!!

With nearly 5 million (a generous guesstimate) homes set to be foreclosed on, are we in need of the banks hoarding this money? Or are we in need of true relief for America? Do you want to be dragged down in this economic vortex or do you want something done to help it?

The average mortgage payment for a home in the United States is a little under 1700 (according to wikianswers.com) and people cant afford these payments anymore. Mainly because as homes go down in value so does overall spending and lending. The banks want to keep their money to stay afloat. The people need to keep their money to stay in their homes and can't afford to spend any extra money on other things that they normally would. This is because of the fear of losing their jobs, their homes, their money, and not being able to afford what they already have. To summarize banks have billions of dollars from the government to share with the people, but they are not doing that. People are struggling to keep their homes, their cars, their jobs, and basically their lives in tact. What is the answer to this? Give more money to people who don't need it? I.E. the banks. Or give the money to the people in America who truly need it?

Here is the middle and lower class bailout plan that <u>will</u> work. This plan will not only work for the middle and lower class but it will also work for the banks, insurance companies, and the whole country.

Bail out the American people that are in foreclosure. Give each person that can not afford their payment a 2 year grant that pays the payment for them for 2 years straight. This way the banks get the money owed to them, the people keep their houses, foreclosures stop, the real estate market doesn't experience the drop in housing prices because the people are now staying and not causing a fire sale (a fire sales is where everything must go and prices are drastically reduced to get the items sold)on homes that would cripple our economy further.

How would we determine who gets assistance and who doesn't? Once this bill is passed, how do we prevent people from taking advantage of it by going into foreclosure just to not to have to make a payment for 2 years. These are just 2 of the questions I asked myself when I came up with this idea. Here are the rules that would prevent this bill from being abused

1. You must be at least 90 days behind on your mortgage and going into foreclosure status.
2. You must prove via income tax records and current pay stubs that you are experiencing a true financial hardship.
3. You can not sell your home during this 2 year period or take out a home equity loan on the property.
4. If after 2 years the people are still unable to afford their home the government would take over the home and sell it at fair market value and not have to fire sale it!! The government recoups its money and nobody gets hurt. The government can hold a property and rent it or sell it with a lot more flexibility than a bank.
5. The money would be distributed directly to the banks via the grant. This would prevent the people from taking the money from the grant and using it for other things and still having the home foreclosed on.

How does this help you might be asking? Like I stated earlier the government is counting on the money trickling down from the banks and companies to reach the people to help them (but like I said earlier this isn't happening, they are keeping it).

My way the banks still get the money owed and the people keep their homes and reestablish their lives. They keep money they would have had to use for 2 years of mortgage payments for other things. I.E. home repairs, cars (thus helping the automobile industry's crisis that they are in), opening small businesses, etc. The next 2 years with no mortgage payment would allow the people to save more for the future and not have to worry about how they are going to make their mortgage payment next month or the month after or the one after that. It gives piece of mind for a short time, but during that time our economy rebounds thanks to the influx of money being put to the banks from the government (from the peoples mortgage grant)and thanks to the people spending the money they would normally be trying to save their homes with. Heck, Americans can take part of that money they are saving to get out of debt in other places like credit cards for instance. This would give the banks even more money!!

How much would this cost you might ask? Well let's do the math.

$1700 per month on average (again it is an average some could be less or more) times 24 months, times 5,000,000 homes.

$1700
x 24
$40,800

$40,800
x 5,000,000
$204,000,000,000.

Yep only $204,000,000,000 (204 billion dollars) quite a bit less than the $700 billion that the government already had set aside (of which there is only $350 billion left with nothing to show for the first $350 billion already spent. Well, nothing to show as far as helping get out of this financial crisis that is!!)

So lets take the $204,000,000,000 out of the remaining $350,000,000,000 and actually help the people who need it and help the whole country at the same time (including the banks)!!!

I have shown this analogy to a few people in the past month since I written it and I have gotten the exact same response from every business man, banker, economist, and even a few political people that I have shown it to. That response is this.... "IT WILL NEVER WORK BECAUSE NOT ENOUGH PEOPLE ARE GETTING PAID OFF IN YOUR PLAN." I fully understand what they mean by this. The original "TARP" proposal was only 10-20 pages long. This plan was not approved by congress. However it was approved after many additions were made to the bill. (I am not sure on the total length of the TARP program but I know it is more than 200 pages long thanks to the additions made) For instance one thing that was added was 9 million dollars for bow and arrow research. Yep you read it right bow and arrow research. You know the stuff that Native Americans used to fight the settlers with. Pardon my language here but what the Hell????? Last I checked we are a lot further along in weapons technology than bows and freakin' arrows, aren't we? I used to own a gun myself. I am 100% sure my gun would have beaten a bow and arrow in a fair (or not so fair in this case) fight and I didn't get paid one red cent for that research/common sense.   Where is my million dollars for that insightfullness? Where is my grant to make that study come about? I'll tell you where it is...it is in someone else's back pocket.

I am going to quote a very famous movie here (by the way I will be quoting a lot of movies in this book) the movie is ***INDEPENDENCE DAY***....and I quote "You don't actually think they spend $20,000.00 on a hammer, $30,000.00 on a toilet seat do you?" I truly think that money is going to be used for something else other than bow and arrow research. I have absolutely no idea on what that could possibly be. I am guessing it is lining the pocket of some politician or being used to support his or her own agenda.

Honestly since TARP was passed we have not gotten any results. People are still losing their homes at alarming rates. Unemployment is getting close to 10%. Yep, 10%. That means that of the 300 plus million people in this country, 3 million plus of them are not working. Can we fix this? I believe we can. It is going to take some sacrifice from government, companies, and the American people like you and me.

I know a lot of people will be reading this book after all $700 billion from TARP has already been spent and that includes the last $350 billion that I was counting on for my plan. Well, to that I say, so what. The $204 billion could be found somewhere. This is needed to help our economy and our overall well being as a country.

We as a country are already making sacrifices. We are losing our jobs while politicians keep theirs. We are losing our jobs while CEO'S of companies are making millions of dollars even though their companies are losing money. Americans are still losing their homes and the rich and well off are buying them up so they can rent them back to the people that lost them. (maybe not the same house but you know what I mean.) So because of poor government decisions once again the people that needed the help didn't get it. But the people that didn't need the help got even more money in their pockets. You may be asking yourself what is going to happen when the housing market hits rock bottom? I'll tell you what is going to happen the people that bought all those foreclosed houses are going to be selling them and turning a huge profit. Yet again putting more money in the wealthy folks pockets.

What you just read above was my idea for immediate help to our families in need. If you don't like that plan maybe you will like my next one instead.

I was just reading that the new stimulus package that congress passed is a 15,000 dollar tax credit to first time home buyers and they also want to offer 30 year fixed interest rates of 4% to "qualified" home buyers. That is all fine and dandy for the people that are considering buying homes for the first time and are just renting. What about the 5 million plus people that are losing their homes? What about the people that have already lost their homes? These people are obviously not going to be "qualified"! They are still out on their collective asses. They are still losing or have already lost their home. They are never going to be "qualified" again for a home because of this problem. Maybe not never, but it will be a long time, that is for sure.

The housing crisis didn't just happen to people who got in over their heads. It happened to people that had long term jobs and great careers that got laid off. It happened to families that lived in their homes for over 10 years and had great credit but lost 1 or more of the families incomes, or even took pay cuts just to keep their jobs. These people are working hard and they have tried to make ends meet but just couldn't do it. Most of these people had to take out home equity loans to help refurbish or fix their homes. Lets face it houses need repair all the time and if you can't afford to shell out the money and you have the equity why wouldn't you use it? These are good people that have had bad things happen to them. This could turn into a never ending spiral unless we help these people get homes again. How are we going to do this you might ask? The government needs to set up grants for these people. These grants are for down payments on a house and not just a tax credit. They also need to set up a national lending program for these people that now have bad credit because of this crisis. I am not talking about a government backed loan via a bank. I am talking about the actual federal government being the bank on these loans. I am talking about the mortgage payments being made to the federal government.

If things falter with these loans then the government can adjust the mortgage to help the family. Let's face it the institution with the most money in this country is our government. The only way to get out of the economic crisis we are in is to have our government lend out the money. They need to stop lending it to the banks and other financial institutions and start lending it to the people that need it the most.

I brought this up to one of my co-workers and he said that puts us in a socialist economy and not a capitalist economy. He said it was almost like a communist economy. That is not the case. This isn't about the government owning the homes. It is about the government helping the people that need the help. The people would still own their homes they would just have them mortgaged through the government. The interest would go to our government to lower our deficit and lower our taxes in the long run. One thing that would be taken into account on this is that banks can still purchase these loans from the government if they wish. Right now we have banks buying loans from other banks anyway. (I can't tell you how many times my mortgage was sold to another lender in a 1 year period...it was hard keeping track of where to send the payments)

For arguments sake let's say this new government lending program starts tomorrow, they lend out 150 billion dollars to people that the economy struck hard and are losing their homes or have already lost their homes. The government takes the risk for a couple years (yes only 2 years. That is a drop in the bucket as far as time goes) and after 2 years the banks start buying up these loans. The people would have re-established their good payment history via the government lending program and now the banks won't be taking as big of a risk if they lent out the money in the first place. So in 2 years the government is mostly out of this business. Yes there still will be people that bad things happen to like losing all or some of their income. This program will allow the government to help these people out.

This plan would not be available for the people that are already "qualified" for the 15000 dollar tax credit. This plan is only available to people losing their home or have already lost them. Yes of course their needs to be some rules with it. Like for instance you have to have a job and the home has to be one you can afford with that job. You can use the grant program I talked about earlier for down payment if need be. Which I am sure it would be needed in most cases. This program needs to be put into any stimulus package that congress is considering. Jobs will also be created with this federal lending program because you would need people to over see the whole program and also people will be needed to work with the home owners. It is a win-win situation, which means it won't happen because it makes too much sense and not enough money in it for the politicians.

Our beloved government wants to start a "bad bank". Bad bank is a term for a financial institution created to hold nonperforming assets owned by a federally insured bank. Such institutions have been created to address challenges arising during an economic credit crunch wherein private banks are allowed to take problem assets off their books. (This is according to wikipedia.com)

First we give the banks billions of dollars so they will start loaning again and they didn't do that. Now they want to open this "Bad Bank" and buy up all or some of the bad or "toxic" assets from the very same banks. That means that these banks will give up the bad home mortgages to the "Bad Bank" and this will clean off their balance sheets. Yet another benefit for the banks. When will the benefits for the banks stop? Why should we have to buy up these assets? What will happen with these assets? Will our government still foreclose on these houses? What will be done to help the people instead of the banks.

Here is my idea for a true bad bank. This bad bank will fix the problem and not just put a band-aid over it. The idea is pretty simple. First and foremost forget buying these toxic assets from the banks. Like I stated earlier this will only help the banks. What we need to do is fix the toxic assets instead of just moving them. We need to open a bad bank for people that have bad credit. Give people the opportunity to borrow again. Let the good people in this country that have had bad times happen to them get another chance. Let a person buy a home that needs a home. Like I said earlier there will be an estimated 5 million homes (again a very generously low guesstimate) foreclosed in the year 2009. That is not counting the millions that have already been foreclosed on.

If we truly want to get out of the financial crisis let the true bad bank open. We need to get people in this country to have homes, buy things for those homes, and most of all we need to give our people a second chance. The rules would be simple for this bank.

Rules:

1. Payment can not exceed 20% of the gross household income.
2. Payments must be automatically deducted from your payroll check

3. The total household debt to income ratio can not exceed 40% including new home payment
4. The home must pass a home inspection that would come with a guarantee.
5. No fixer up houses. We want the houses to be affordable and if you have to fix stuff it may add to your debt.

The guarantee that I just suggested above must meet the following requirements:

1. A roof with a guaranteed life expectancy of 10 years.
2. A furnace with a guaranteed life expectancy of 10 years.
3. No termites.
4. No electrical problems.
5. No plumbing problems.

I am sick of our government helping the big businesses and banks. This program will allow the people that are actually in need of help to get the help they need. And by following all of these guidelines I truly believe we can rebuild peoples lives and get our economy back to where it belongs.

You just read 3 examples of things that can be done to help people that are having their houses foreclosed upon or have already had their houses foreclosed on. I think these are not only good solutions but they are also viable solutions. They could easily be put into affect and it would help our country more than any bills that congress passes in the future and would do it for a lot less too.

Our new President is trying to make this all work out, but he is missing the big picture, and here is proof.

The date is February 18th, 2009. President Obama just announced his plan to help home owners. Here is his "answer"(as posted by CNN.com on February 18th, 2009)...

President Obama is unveiling a $75 billion multi-pronged plan Wednesday that seeks to help up to 9 million borrowers suffering from falling home prices and unaffordable monthly payments.

The long-awaited foreclosure fix marks a sharp departure from the Bush administration, which relied mainly on having servicers voluntarily modify troubled mortgages.

Obama, meanwhile, will make it easier homeowners to afford their monthly payments either by refinancing the mortgages or having their loans modified. The president is vastly broadening the scope of the government rescue by focusing on homeowners who are still current in their payments but at risk of default. And he puts billions of federal funds into enticing servicers to modify the loans of those who've already stopped paying.

The program contains a mix of carrots and sticks for mortgage servicers and investors, both of whom have been seen as resistant to modifying loans. The program would not only give servicers $1,000 for each modification, but would give them another $1,000 a year for three years if the borrower stays current. It will also give $500 to servicers and $1,500 to mortgage holders if they modify at-risk loans before the borrower falls behind.

But the administration is also wielding a big stick. It will work with Congress to amend bankruptcy laws to allow judges to modify mortgages, a step community advocates say is badly needed but that the financial industry abhors.

"In the end, all of us are paying a price for this home mortgage crisis," Obama was expected to say in a speech Wednesday. "And all of us will pay an even steeper price if we allow this crisis to deepen -- a crisis which is unraveling homeownership, the middle class, and the American Dream itself. But if we act boldly and swiftly to arrest this downward spiral, every American will benefit."

The Obama plan calls for:

- *Helping borrowers who owe more than 80% of their home's value to refinance and reduce their monthly payments.*

- *Creating a $75 billion homeowner stability initiative to reduce monthly payments for at-risk borrowers by subsidizing interest rates. The goal would be to bring payments to no more than 31% of a borrower's income.*

- *Providing multiple incentives to servicers to modify loans and to proactively help at-risk borrowers while they are still current in their payments.*

- *Creating a $10 billion fund to protect investors and servicers against further home price declines.*

- *Requiring all financial institutions receiving government funds to participate in a standardized loan modification program, while seeking to have all federal agencies that own or guarantee loans also apply the guidelines.*

- *Allowing judges to modify mortgages during bankruptcy, a measure the financial industry has strongly opposed.*

- *Providing more Treasury Department backing of Fannie Mae and Freddie Mac and expanding the number of mortgages the agencies back*

I almost like this. The key word is almost. He is basically helping 9 million people that are struggling to make ends meet. That is the good thing. The bad thing is the average amount of that "help" is just a little over 8000 dollars per borrower. How is this going to help anyone? It is like putting a band-aid over a gunshot wound, the bleeding may never stop at this point. It is just not going to be enough to help the people that really need it. Come on! Wake up already! 8000 dollars? That isn't even 700 dollars per month for one year. And what if that 8000 dollars is spread out over a longer period of time than just one year? What if it is spread out over the remaining time of your loan? So, thank you Mr. President for lowering my mortgage payment almost 17 dollars per month for the next 20 years.

He is also going to provide multiple "incentives" to mortgage servicers to modify loans and to proactively help at-risk borrowers while they are still current on their payments. So if you are still current you can refinance. No shit, Dick Tracy, that is common sense. If you are current that means your credit is still good and you can refinance anyway. I didn't need a government backed program to tell me that people that have good credit and are not late on their payments can refinance. If you have good credit you can still get a home too. What about the people that have bad credit because they are behind on their payments right now? Oh, wait! It says that those people can mess up their credit even more and file bankruptcy and the judge will be allowed to modify that loan. Fantastic, isn't it? So now your credit is bad because of your mortgage and instead of our government helping you (like they did for so many banks and other corporations that are in trouble.) get caught up and get your credit back on track we are going to make you file bankruptcy and you might as well take all of your creditors down in that bankruptcy too. This way you can keep your house but you won't be able to get credit for anything else for a very long time.

I was just referring to other creditors that have bankruptcy filed on them because why would you only file bankruptcy on just the home. Any good bankruptcy attorney will tell you that if you are going to file bankruptcy take anyone down you can. What do you think that is going to do to the economy? I will tell what it is going to do. It is going to cause an even bigger ripple effect. Think about it...if I file bankruptcy and take my credit cards down with me, that means those banks are not going to get payments from me. That means that the banks lose that money. And doesn't that hurt our economy? According to what is happening right now I believe that it does indeed hurt our economy. This is not helping at all. I know his heart is in the right place when he came up with this legislation but start using your brain Mr. President and stop listening to people that got us into this trouble in the first place.

I was just reading another article about Obama's homeowner rescue plan. This article was published on February 20th, 2009.

By STEVENSON JACOBS and ALAN ZIBEL, AP Business Writers Stevenson Jacobs And Alan Zibel,

NEW YORK – Banks got bailed out. So did automakers. So why not struggling homeowners? The question has struck a raw nerve across the country, with critics saying the Obama administration's latest housing rescue rewards people who bought homes they couldn't afford. Others counter that the taxpayer-financed plan will slow spiraling home prices and avert a deeper economic disaster.

The debate captures the strong emotions stirred up over who benefits as the government tries to fix the financial crisis. It's likely to remain on the front burner for months as lawmakers consider other contentious issues — like whether bankruptcy judges should be given the power to impose changes on borrowers' home loans.

"I feel like I'm doing the right thing paying my mortgage, and now apparently I have to pay my neighbor's mortgage, too. People are really angry," said Kim Guymon, a stay-at-home mom who bought a three-bedroom home with her husband in suburban Seattle in 2001 and has watched it drop $150,000 in value since last summer.

Rescuing people whose homes are worth less than they own on their mortgages doesn't sit well with Robert Bechler, either. Still, the 37-year-old flooring contractor said he sees little choice.

"If they don't bail those people out, it's just going to get worse. It's a necessary evil, I suppose," said Bechler, who with his fiancée just bought a house in Cape Coral, Fla. for $92,000 after waiting years for prices to fall.

The rescue plan unveiled Wednesday by President Barack Obama offers $75 billion in incentives for banks and investors to reduce struggling home borrowers' interest rates and make other changes to loan terms. The money will *come from the second half the $700 billion federal financial bailout. The goal is to keep 4 million homeowners out of foreclosure and halt free-falling home prices.*

To qualify, lenders and mortgage investors would have to agree on a lower interest rate that would be designed to reduce the borrower's mortgage payments to 38 percent of their pretax income. The government would then provide financing to bring that ratio down to 31 percent.

Another piece is designed to help borrowers who are still making their payments on time, but want to refinance into lower mortgage rates.

Republican lawmakers and conservative pundits immediately denounced the plan as an affront to free market principles and said it promotes irresponsible borrowing.

Rep. Jeb Hensarling, a Texas Republican, summed up the plan as "Nice guys finish last." Conservative columnist David Brooks echoed those sentiments in a New York Times column titled "Money for Idiots."

Rick Santelli, a reporter for financial network CNBC, compared the government's actions to those of communist Cuba during a dramatic, televised rant Thursday from the floor of the Chicago Mercantile Exchange.

"The government is promoting bad behavior, America!" he said.

Video of the exchange has been viewed over 1.2 million times on CNBC.com, more than any other clip in the Web site's history.

Supporters of the plan are pushing back.

"This is the financial equivalent of what Hurricane Katrina did to New Orleans. Did they know they were

living below sea level? Yes. Does that mean we shouldn't help them? That's ridiculous," said Kathleen Day of the nonprofit Center For Responsible Lending.

In an interview with The Associated Press, Obama's housing secretary, Shaun Donovan, said it's in everyone's interest to stop the wave of foreclosures, which drag down the prices of all homes in an affected area.

"What we're doing is we're benefiting everybody," he said.

Donovan said administration officials considered the potential backlash from angry borrowers when they designed the plan. That's why it doesn't just help borrowers in danger of losing their homes, he said. It also aims to make it easier for households who owe more on their mortgages than their homes are worth to refinance. There are nearly 14 million households in that situation, according to Moody's Economy. com.

In the coming months Congress is poised to try to hash out a set of housing issues, including whether the bankruptcy change is needed and a proposal to protect companies that collect mortgage payments from investor lawsuits.

The tussle over the housing bailout comes as the government is doling out hundreds of billions in bailouts and stimulus for banks, Detroit automakers and recession-weary consumers.

So why has the housing bailout wound up so many people?

Part of it has to do with the critical role housing plays in the national identity, said Barry Ritholtz, a financial analyst and author of "Bailout Nation, How Corrupt money Shook Wall Street."

"The average family doesn't have a huge stock portfolio. But you have 100 million families that own homes," Ritholtz said.

Rosa Valdez, a resident of Coachella, Calif., hopes it's not too late for her family to be helped. The native of Mexico saved enough to buy a new $380,000 home in 2006 in the Lennar development of La Morada, where foreclosures are rampant. She fears her home could be next without federal help.

"It's our last resource," said Valdez, who was turned down when she tried to renegotiate her loan.

O.B. Brock of Charleston, W. Va., opposes bailing out people who got in over their heads and the banks that helped them.

"It's just rewarding crooks," said the 38-year-old single mother, who said she turned down a bank's $100,000 mortgage offer five years ago because she knew she couldn't afford it.

Others are more sympathetic.

Debra Rodriguez, of Tucson, said she believes many borrowers were victimized by unscrupulous lenders.

"I could sit back and say 'Hey, I'm not getting anything and that's not fair.' But I've been fortunate enough that I don't need a bailout," Rodriguez said.

For Chris Grande of suburban Dayton, Ohio, helping troubled borrowers only makes sense after the billions spent on other bailouts.

"Does it reward bad behavior? Absolutely, it does. But no more than the banks who offered these loans rewarding themselves for their own bad behavior," said Grande, 26.

That is probably one of the most interesting articles I have read about this plan because it shows some examples of how some American's feel about this plan. Some people get it and some people don't get it. I really like the lady that said she was against the program because she was doing the right thing by paying her mortgage and now she has to pay her neighbor's too and doesn't think that is fair? She also states that she has watched her house value drop 150,000 dollars in less than a year. Well duh!! Hey lady why do you think your house value dropped? It is because one of your neighbor's houses got foreclosed on and the bank has to unload it so they are pricing it to sell. That price will be less than your houses value so that means your house goes down in value as well. So if our government doesn't step in and help these people out your house is going to keep dropping in value and you will lose even more money. Basically, by our government helping these homeowners out they are helping people that are not in trouble by keeping the housing market from getting saturated even further with over 5 million homes that are going to be foreclosed on.

This is the "I am holier than thou" attitude that I see happening all too often in this country. "It is not my fault. I don't care about my fellow countryman down the street. I didn't do it so why should I have to help anyone else besides myself." This is how it is with my kids right now. Anytime something happens or a mess gets made it is the " I didn't do it so why should I have to fix it or clean it up?" attitude. Maybe it is because it is the right thing to do. As I have pointed out numerous times in this chapter if we help these people out we help everyone in the long run.

I really liked what Kathleen Day of the non profit Center for Responsible Lending said. She was right. Would we not help people out, the people in New Orleans after Katrina, just because they knew they lived in an area that could possibly flood? Of course we would never do that. Those people needed help and got it or are getting it still to this day. People were buying houses based on the values of houses going up and continually going up. They never anticipated this economic crisis so why not use everything at our disposal to help us all out?

I personally am having a hard time understanding the banks actual philosophy when it comes to not negotiating a refinance for people in trouble. When they foreclose on a home they have to sit on it and hope to sell it. Most of the time they wind up selling the house for much less than the loan balance. Of course this also takes time to sell it and it takes money to advertise it. Not to mention the fact that they are also paying a commission to a Realtor to sell it. So let me summarize the foreclosure situation from the banks perspective:

1. Turn down people living in house for refinance or renegotiation of current loan.
2. Start foreclosure procedures.
3. Foreclose on home and kick people out to the street.
4. Contact real estate agency to sell home.
5. Do repairs to home so they can sell home.
6. Wait to sell home.

7. Finally sell home for big loss.

Does this truly make sense? If the banks actually renegotiated these loans they would make the money not lose it. People would keep their homes not lose them. We would not be in the economic crisis that we are in right now. Our government would not have to bail out these banks for billions upon billions of dollars.

Do I think what President Obama is doing is enough? HELL NO!! 75 billion is no where near enough to get these homeowners the help they need. But it is a start!! And we do have to start somewhere. I still think my plan will wind up costing less than anything that we are doing right now.

There are a lot more things wrong with our economy than just housing. However housing right now is one of the biggest but there are some more like...

Downsizing!! Downsizing is yet another thing that is happening in our country that is hurting our economy. Did you know that CEO's are laying people off just so they can keep their bonuses? That is the American way. Cutting jobs is the easiest way to increase your bottom line. A little common sense here people. How the hell can these companies justify paying millions upon millions of dollars to these guys for failure? I make a mistake at my job and I have 3 people up my ass telling me what I did wrong yet again and nobody is getting fired so I can keep my salary or bonus. I guarantee if you and I lost our companies money like these morons have we would have been out on our collective asses. If I am on the board of directors of these companies this is the first thing I would ask "Excuse me Mr. Shithead CEO, this company is paying you millions of dollars to run this company and make all of us directors and our stock holders money but you lost us millions (even billions in some cases) of dollars instead. Why should you keep your job? Why shouldn't you be the first person to be let go? You want to cut thousands of our work force to increase our bottom line but I think we could increase our bottom line by letting one person go. YOU!!" How is that for common sense?

I personally work on a commission basis. (Oh crap...I forgot to tell you that I work in the automobile industry. I am a finance manager. I am the guy that is seeing car loans get turned down an awful lot lately)That means if I make the company money, I make myself money. If I don't make money for my company, I don't get paid!! Pretty simple don't you think? How can we not adopt this for the leaders of these companies? You want to get paid 2 million dollars a year as head of this company you better make this company 50 million dollars. I think a 4% commission would be fair for these guys. Sign them up to an average based salary and then commission the rest to them. Give them lets say an average base of 100000 dollars and 4% commission. That way they get some money to pay everyday expenses. But, if they want to make millions then the companies they work for need to make millions upon millions of dollars. I am sick of seeing these CEO's and VP's getting rich while the employees are getting laid off. Come on American companies start getting what you pay for. If you pay someone millions of dollars to run your company, you should not be losing money, you should be making money.

The year 2008 will go down in history as one of the worst times in Wall Street history. That is unless you are an executive on Wall Street. The total bonuses paid out to employees of financial companies in New York was an estimated 18.4 billion dollars. That was the sixth largest bonus payout total in history. Some of the bankers took home millions of dollars in the year 2008 even as their companies lost billions. The New York state comptroller, Thomas P. DiNapoli, is not sure if any or all of that money came from the taxpayer bailout or not. According to Mr. DiNapoli, the brokerage companies of New York lost 35 billion dollars in 2008. Correct me if I am wrong but aren't bonuses supposed to be paid for doing a great, or heck, even a good job. Does losing 35 billion dollars constitute doing a good job? If it does I am really going to be rich because I lost 10 bucks that I can't seem to find anywhere so that must mean that I am going to get 100,000 of taxpayer money. Woo hoo for me!!

Let's take a look at what money has been paid out of the $350 billion so far. (According to wikipedia.com on January 29, 2009.)

Citigroup got $50 billion

Bank of America got $45 billion

AIG got $40 billion

JP Morgan Chase got $25 billion

GM got $13.4 billion

Goldman Sachs got $10 billion

Morgan Stanley got $10 billion

PNC Financial Services Group got $7.579 billion

U.S. Bancorp got $6.6 billion

GMAC Financial Services got $5 billion

Chrysler got $4 billion

Capital One Financial got $3.555 billion

American Express got $3.389 billion

That gives a grand total of 223.523 billion dollars of the first 350 billion gone. It also leaves 126.477 billion dollars that has not been reported to the public. Where did that money go? 126.477 billion dollars missing? Over one third of the 350 billion dollars. Whose pocket is that lining? What other stupid things did we pay for out of this money? I mean besides bows and arrows that is? I think since TARP is paying this money to these companies we should know where it is going and where it has gone.

Now some of the 223.523 million dollars that went to these companies actually went to purchase stocks in these companies. This 700 billion dollars is coming from our tax payer money. That means we Americans technically own part of these companies. So when these companies pay out dividends to stock holders do we get a share? When the companies actually buy back these stocks from the government do we get our money back? What if these companies suddenly rebound tremendously and start turning a profit and the stocks go up do we get our money back plus the profits? So if after all is said and done and the 700 billion dollar investment we as taxpayers put forth turns a profit of lets say 350 billion dollars do we all get our money back plus 1000 extra in return for our investment? (350 billion dollars divided by 350 million people equals 1000 each). I think that these are really good questions that I would like answers to.

In a Newsweek article published January 19, 2009, Bank of America CEO Kenneth D. Lewis is quoted as saying "it's not a one-to-one relationship, we don't write 15 billion dollars in loans because we got 15 billion dollars from the government." In this same article banking CEO's defend what is going on. They believe the government funds are designed to shore up capital and support lending but they have absolutely no obligation to make new loans to help the economy. EXCUSE ME? That is exactly what the American people were told was going to happen when TARP was being passed. Banks are getting billions of dollars to help the economy by being able to lend again, and all they are doing with this money is helping themselves and keeping this money. We are getting robbed. The only difference is that these guys are doing it in broad daylight with no masks on and no guns. And, they are doing it all legally. Yes, this is all legal, because our government didn't put any kind of stipulations on this money. They never had these banks sign anything that said here is how this money must be used. They were just handed over the cash and the government basically walked away. That is like giving your 5 year old son 100 dollars at the local WalMart and tell him that it is his money and he can use it for whatever he wants but maybe he should get his grandma a birthday card and get her a birthday gift too from that money. Sure your son might buy a card for 5 dollars and a small gift like a 5 dollar bottle of perfume. And I am willing to bet the rest of the money will get spent on Nintendo games, candy, and toys. Did he do something wrong in this scenario? Nope. You said it was his money and he did do what you thought he should do with it. But he spent more on himself. And that was never stipulated as wrong. So how can we punish the banks for taking this money and doing what they want with it? I say that they have to show where every dollar that the government gives you is going and how it is spent. If you do not comply you must give that money back to the government and you will not receive any more of the tax payers money

There are other things that are hurting our economy as well. Let me tell you what I have seen. I have seen people that moved here from Poland. Lived here for about 10 years. Worked here during that entire time. Saved money for 10 years and moved back to Poland and live like royalty. The American dollar is worth a lot there as opposed to here. And the cost of living is a lot less than here too. By doing this, money is taken from the retailers here. This causes job losses here. Money is taken from here via the salaries paid to these people and then the money is not spent here. Instead it is being spent in another country. Do you think this is a drain on our economy? I sure as hell do.

Here is another thing that is happening right under our noses. People that have immigrated here are buying things on credit and making a few payments and then skipping off back to their home country with all the stuff and not having to pay for it. I have run many a credit report where the people have over 100000 dollars of credit card debt and plan on moving back to their homeland in a short period of time. Tell me our banks are not suffering because of this and I will call you a liar and a moron.

How do I know this is happening? Well let me tell you how I know. I deal with a lot of people in my job. I deal with Polish, Russian, Hispanic, and as a matter of fact working where I work and doing what I do, it is almost like working at the U.N. Building itself because of the amount of diversity I have coming through my office. If it is happening in my office how many other places do you think it is happening? I am saying it is happening more than we think.

We just had a situation just like this happen to our dealership. We had some people that moved here from Poland and lived here for a few years. They built up their credit and had a great credit score. They came to us and bought a 50,000 hybrid vehicle with no money down. And that was the last we heard from them. But not the last we heard about them. A few months later our lenders representative came in and told us that these people skipped out on them. And not just them but the same week they purchased that 50,000 vehicle from us they had also bought 4 other vehicles from other dealerships and skipped out on all of those loans too. Now this isn't proven but my lender thinks that these people took all 5 of these vehicles back over to Poland. He thinks that they created fake vehicle titles for all 5 vehicles. So here are 5 lenders that are out approximately 150,000 dollars. (I think that estimate might be low too!) What happens to those lenders? Do you think that this scenario might have an effect on our economy? I certainly do. We need laws in place that prevent this from happening. At the very least we need a law that holds the shipping yard responsible for checking to make sure the title is true and free and clear of all liens. I am sure they can set it up at these shipping yards to have the shipping company check all the important information about the vehicle.

The other thing I am seeing is that these same people are buying cars here in America and taking them back overseas legally, not just the way I just described above. You are probably asking why would they be doing this? Well of course I am going tell you why. They are buying the cars here and selling them there for twice the value. They are buying 20,000 dollar cars here and selling them there for the equivalent of 40,000 dollars. That is pretty smart on their part but it hurts our economy. How does this hurt our economy you might be asking. They are still spending money here right? They are buying our products and selling them over seas right? Well, think about that for a second. If they are buying our products and shipping them overseas to sell for a 100% profit who is losing that profit? Our car companies are losing that profit. Our car companies have dealerships over there just like they do here. The car that is in a dealership there is selling the same car for maybe the equivalent of 45000. Even though they are selling the car here for the 20000 they are losing that 25000 difference. If people are buying the cars here for half the price, and then selling them over there they keep the money not the American company! They lose that sale! They lose that extra money they would have gained by exporting that car to those countries. Profit is profit and I am all for American companies making as much as they can from other countries because that means more jobs for us here (screw the other country and their jobs) and more money going to other companies and banks here thus helping our economy. That is all we should care about, our economy. Nobody else's economy , just ours. Let them worry about their own instead of ours. Oh wait, they already do that.

Here is another idea to help my industry and our economy at the same time. Have our government give 5000 dollars to car dealers for every car 10 years and older. This will also help our environment. There are obviously cars that are worth more than 5000 dollars that are 10 years old...like classic cars, muscle cars, etc. but those people will not want to get rid of them anyway, so no biggie. Could you imagine how many new cars our country would sell if the people that have a 10 year old car got an automatic 5000 dollars for their old pieces of crap? Imagine how much that would help the economy. This would even help the credit crunch too because it would give these people an automatic 5000 dollar down payment. Picture this...you own a 1998 Chevy Berretta, it is falling apart. You go look at a new car that has a sticker price of 20,000 dollars. Without this program his trade in would be worth maybe 500 bucks. That leaves 19500 dollars plus tax license and title to pay for either via finance or cash. My way there is only 15,000 dollars as a balance. That would help put banks in a great equity position and more willing to loan money out without fear of losing their collective asses if they did have to repossess it, God forbid.

There will obviously have to be a lot of stipulations on this process. For instance the people would have to buy a car 4 years old or newer. The dealer can not resell the traded in cars to other consumers. And here is how we prevent these cars from being resold and creating the problem all over again. The government actually gives this money to the car dealers and in exchange the car dealers give the cars to the government to have them destroyed. By doing this it would also create jobs at wrecking yards throughout the country. It would also help keep jobs in the automakers factories. Our government wants to give money to people that need it. This is just one example of how that would be happen.

Speaking of keeping jobs in America....

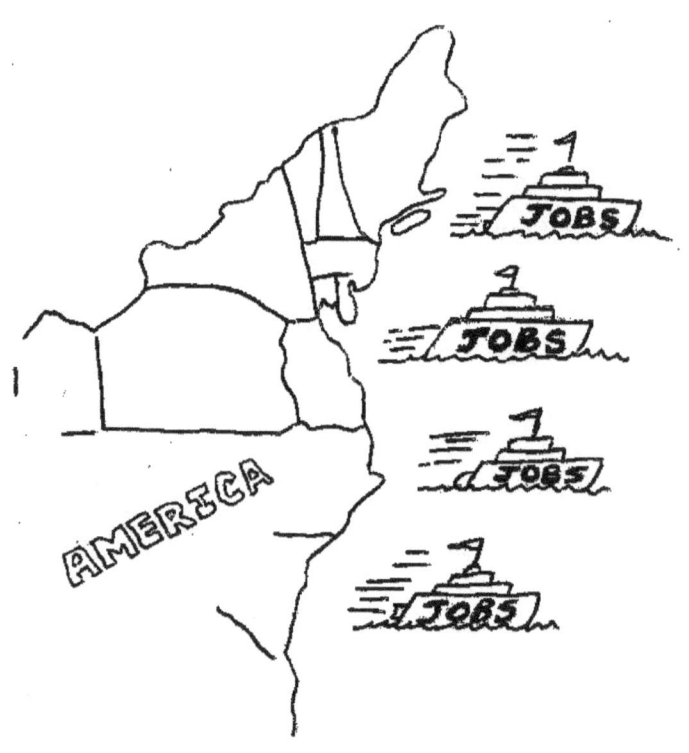

AMERICAN COMPANIES

The American Company is falling apart. People are losing jobs to other countries as well as just plain losing them. I remember a day when made in America meant something. I would like to have it mean something again. Without the American Companies we as a nation can not survive.

In the previous chapter, I have already talked about how CEO's of companies (that includes the Big Three automakers in Detroit) are getting paid a Hell of a lot of money to not make any money for their companies or stock holders. I still don't get it. I don't think I ever will get it. Getting rid of these multimillionaires is my first step to making the American companies more profitable. I spoke earlier of sacrifices that needed to be made this would be one of them. If you don't get rid of them, at the very least, pay them only if the company makes money.

My next step to fixing the American company will actually help with the American economy as well. **BRING THE JOBS BACK TO THE U.S. Of A!!!** Once again a very simple solution that has been overlooked. We are talking about 10% unemployment yet our companies are outsourcing our jobs to other countries. Why, you may ask, are we doing this? To increase the bottom line. You see other countries people won't make as much money as an American worker will for doing the same job because it costs less to live in the other country so our companies don't have to pay the worker more than what he truly needs to survive in that country. (That is called cost of living. People get paid by the area that they live in.) I will scream at the top of my lungs here!! SCREW THE OTHER COUNTRIES!!! Yep, you read it right.... SCREW EM!! How many people reading this book have called for customer service at their computer company, their phone company, or any company now a days and you here a foreign accent on the line? I will give you a perfect example of this problem.

Two weeks ago I had a problem with my INTERNET service provider. I won't name any names but it starts with the first letter of our alphabet. But like I said, I won't name any names here. So anyway, I called up the 800 number that appeared on my screen that said call for assistance. This is what I heard (in a voice I can only associate with Apu from "The Simpsons" cartoon television show on FOX TV) "Hello, My name is James Smith, what is your name please?" to which I responded "My name is Elvis Presley!!" "Your name is not Elvis Presley" Apu stated. To which I retorted "Your name isn't James Smith either. So you tell me your real name and I will tell you mine." It was right after that statement I heard a click followed by a dial tone. Like I stated earlier my stories are 100% true and I know some of you people have experienced this exact scenario. I couldn't possibly be the only person in this country to live through this fiasco. This is happening way too often. Our jobs are being sent overseas to save a buck or two. I remember when made in America actually meant something. Now days it means that it was assembled here but manufactured somewhere else.

Manufacturing plants and customer service is not the only thing we are outsourcing here. I know a person that works at an MRI clinic near my place of employment. The costs have gotten so high here in the United States that it is actually cheaper to send the images to India and have a radiologist read them there and send back the results to them here. What the Hell is that all about? We are now outsourcing our medical jobs? Who's ass is on the line if they misread them? How do we know they are right? Do we have to have a second opinion done here or do we have to go to another clinic and have them send it over to India to a different radiologist? What if the person over there isn't a true radiologist and is just some goof making the equivalent of 10 dollars an hour there and he has no more than a high school education with some basic training reading these MRI's? I am sure that India's qualifications to be a nurse, doctor, radiologist, and any other medical personnel are not as strict as they are here. Like I said, how do we know?

Here is how we fix our companies. (besides the CEO's getting paid accordingly.) The government gives tax incentives to our American companies to put the jobs where they belong. Back in America! The money that the government would "lose" in these tax incentives would easily be made back up by the income taxes they would get from the salaries of the employees of these companies.

Not to mention this money that the American worker is making in America will now be spent in America at other American retailers creating more sales tax money, more jobs at retailers, and just overall more money flowing into our economy.

Once again I bounced this off of a few people I know and the response I get is mixed. I get these statements "American people won't work for what the foreign countries people will work for!" These so called low paying jobs are better than nothing. Some people in this country are either not working or are working and making very little. Haven't you ever heard of "you have to crawl before you can walk"?

And here is where the tax incentives for the companies comes in also. See if companies get a break to keep the jobs here they will do just that and the pay will be based on the American pay scale and not the overseas scale. What if that is not enough you might be asking? Well, there is another side to this statement. Not only do we give a tax incentive to the companies to get the jobs back here, we will also need to tax the ever living shit out of the companies that keep outsourcing overseas. You don't want to pay the American worker to work for you here? Then you will have to pay the American people back for the loss of that job. So either way our economy gets a boost. That is like a double incentive for American companies to keep the jobs here.

I am an American business owner. I see I can pay someone in India 40 dollars a day or I can pay an American worker 70 dollars a day for doing the same job. Which way should I go? I can't blame the companies for doing this right now the way our system is set up. I would do it too. Now let's do it my way. I can pay an American worker 70 dollars per day to do this job or I can send the job overseas and pay them 40 a day, but oh crap, I have to pay 50 in outsourcing tax to the government. Based on that scenario I lose 20 per day which means I lose 7300 dollars per year for just this one job. And I have over 100 jobs like this. That is going to cost me 730,000 dollars this year. What would that American business owner do now? I know if I were in charge I would keep those 100 jobs here, that is for sure.

I have been asked "What if they just move their factories, customer service, or just plain operations overseas?" This is simple we tax the hell out of anything they import back here. You want to do business here in America you have to help our economy thrive, not be a drag on it. One way or another we will get our money from you. Americans are the largest consumers on this planet. We are the heart and soul of most economies, especially our own. We need to start taking control and not be pushed around by businesses. If not for our people buying and using their products they wouldn't exist so time to start being part of the solution and not part of the problem.

Another statement I get is "Diplomatically you can't do that to the other countries of this world. That isn't right!! Those people in India, Japan, China, etc. need those jobs to help themselves and their families." I have said it before and I know I will say it again - SCREW EM!!! They don't give a rat's ass about us over in these other countries, regardless of what they say at the United Nations meetings or to our media for that matter. Every other country on this planet puts their people first and America last. (They actually don't put their people first either. The other countries put their greed first.) Americans, on the other hand, have to be politically correct. We have to support them. Once again - SCREW EM!!! We need help with our economy and where are they? Are these other countries lining up to save us? A resounding NO on both counts!! Some countries are buying up some of our companies stock because they know those companies will turn around. Yes this helps put money in our economy for the short term, but when these companies start making money again (and they will) what happens with that profit? It goes overseas!! That again starts the cycle of money not being used here to help create more jobs. Once again not much help for us is there?

Here is yet another response to my SCREW EM mentality when it comes jobs here. This statement throws me for a real loop too. The statement is "You are talking about low level, entry level, positions that are being filled overseas. You know grunt work, shitty jobs that don't involve a lot of skill to do. American people want more in their jobs!" I agree with this statement to a point. I think that every career starts somewhere.

I once dated a girl in high school whose father started working for his company fresh out of high school and was still working there 20 plus years later. When he started there he was nothing more than a glorified janitor. At the time I was dating his daughter he was a Vice President of that company. That means he earned respect and he showed what kind of man he was by starting out where he did. We have all of these kids coming out of high school and college and they just think things will be handed to them because they got good grades or because they think they deserve it. Well tough shit junior. You need to crawl before you can walk. Yes your education is worth something but that is just book smarts. You need real world experience and the only way to get that is to experience the real world. Once again I say you must crawl before you can walk. Remember *NATIONAL LAMPOON'S VACATION*? Remember cousin Eddie? I remember how Clark and Helen Griswold talking about Eddie not having a job for many years and she said Eddie's wife Catherine said "he is holding out for a management position". How many people out there in our country are doing that you think? Given the times we are in now how many of those people would take an entry level position?

We have people on welfare and unemployment benefits that could be working and bettering their situation. I have no problems with people that are on welfare. I believe it is necessary sometimes, but sometimes people take advantage of it. The same goes for unemployment. You want these benefits you need to at least try and get a job. I don't care if you go to a job interview to be a ditch digger you need to at least attempt to get off your ass. I still look in the paper and see help wanted all over. Are they great jobs? No. Are the jobs that are available your dream jobs? No. Are they better than nothing? YES!! Maybe they are not enough to make ends meet but maybe if you work and have welfare supplement the difference you will be better off in the long run and once again you may get promoted and get a raise and be able to make ends meet without help. Then you may even keep getting promoted and raises and once again you will be better off. You can't get promoted or get a raise by sitting at home collecting checks.

There is a right way to do things and a wrong way. The perfect example of this is the fact that I currently work for a man that started out doing grunt work at the dealership. He was doing just about anything his father or uncle told him to do. (His father and uncle own the dealership I work for and the son who is the GM now.) My boss started out cleaning cars, he sold cars, fixed cars, and he even did my job. I thank God I am good at what I do or he could easily fire me and replace me with himself. Now that is real world experience. He is one of the best employers (if not the best) I have every worked for. He respects me and all of his employees because he has been there done that and knows what we go through on a daily basis. He treats us equally whenever he can. Yes, he is still my boss and demands that respect. But it isn't so much of a demanded respect as it is an earned respect. That is a man that you want to work for because he earned everything he has. The funniest part about it is he could have coasted through life being the son of a car dealer and had it all handed to him but his father wouldn't allow that to happen. He made him earn it. And earn it he did.

Speaking of earing your own way and earning respect. I am going to tell you what I did when I was younger. When I was 10 - 15 years old I would go around in the summer with my lawnmower and cut peoples grass for 5 or 10 dollars depending on the size of the lawn. In the winter time I would take a shovel around and shovel the sidewalks and the driveways of these same people for 5 or

10 dollars. After awhile I was able to afford a snowblower and I would get more done and made more money, and that is what it was all about. I would bust my butt doing this so I could play video games at the local arcade or go buy slurpees at 7-11. Where is that today? I have owned a home for 15 out of the last 17 years and I have never, ever had a kid come up to my door and ask me if he could cut my lawn or shovel my walk or driveway. Not one!! When I was 13 I actually worked as a dishwasher for a teenage non-alcohol serving bar or juice bar as it has been called, on Friday and Saturday nights until almost 2 am (I know there are laws against that now but that isn't the point I am trying to make). I wasn't making much but I got to meet a lot of people doing that. I had fun doing it and earned my own money for spending. After that I got a work permit and worked at a donut shop on the weekends and a fish fry at a local Eagles club on Friday nights. Then when I finally turned 16 I got a job earning 3.85 per hour at a locally owned grocery store. I worked there until I was 18. Kids today are getting things handed to them by their parents and they don't have to earn it.

Where is this in today's world? Let me tell you where it is...it is in these foreign countries. These "3rd world" countries are taking these "low level" jobs and turning it into experience they use for a real career later in life. That is the way it used to be here and that is the way it should be here now.

Kids today want it all handed to them. They want everything from their parents hard work. They want to coast into college where they think it is some hard studying and harder partying. We need our children to get the feel of real life and real work whenever possible. They need to see that everything is not handed to them. You need to show who you are and what you are made of . Right now kids today are made of McDonald's and video games. Not hard work and determination.

Speaking of getting stuff handed to you. Unions are another thing that need to be reformed. The UAW, The Teamsters, and most other unions (but those are 2 of the more famous ones) are causing this outsourcing that is going on. Back in the day you negotiated some great contracts for your members and that is great. Nobody can fault you for that. However now your people are being laid off and outsourced. (Or worse yet insourced. Insourced means that people that are immigrants come here and take our jobs and make less money but do the same job. Insourced was taken from the movie *SWING VOTE* starring Kevin Costner) The worst part about that is that you are allowing it. You would rather see your people get laid off or lose their jobs all together rather than make some necessary concessions and cutbacks of your own. Once again nobody can fault you for wanting more for your members and wanting to have them make the most money that they possibly can. However, I would rather make some money as opposed to no money. And that is what is happening here. People are getting laid off and making less than what they are making now and in some cases these people are making nothing at all. How does that benefit your members?

Another interesting clause of the UAW contracts is the 30 years of service and retire program. Yep, 30 years of working and you can retire. If you start working for the UAW at 18 you could conceivably retire at the age of

48 with full benefits that include full health care and a pension. The average life expectancy of a person today is over 70. That means that this same person that started working at 18 could collect all these benefits for almost as long as they actually worked for the company. Now granted most people are not starting work at age 18 for the big 3 in Detroit but some are starting at 21, 22, etc. that still gives them quite a long time of full retirement benefits.

Here is the problem with GM, Chrysler, Ford, and even the UAW. They are afraid of everything that is going on. The Big 3 are afraid of the UAW striking because that would cost billions. The UAW officers are afraid of not being reelected to their cushy jobs if they lessen any of these benefits to their members. Someone needs to step up here or our government needs to step in and get things back in line. The interesting part about this is that if the Big 3 file bankruptcy it will void the UAW contracts. They will start all over from scratch. I am sure the UAW doesn't want that. I know the Big 3 doesn't want to have to do that because it would take a lot more effort on their part to get things were they need to be.

Now once again I must explain I am not a Rhodes scholar here. I am not an economist either. I am a regular citizen that knows only what he reads, sees, and researches. And believe me I researched a lot for this book. With that being said I just watched a FOX news special on what the UAW contract is costing our American car companies. And I am shocked at the difference.

For instance I just watched this analyst state that for Toyota 200 dollars of the cars cost goes toward medical benefits for their employees. Whereas 1500 dollars of the cost of a GM car goes toward medical benefits and retiree's. Yes part of the UAW contract is that even the retirees are entitled to full benefits as if they are still working for GM, Chrysler, and Ford. Isn't that what Medicare is for? Now I know Medicare doesn't pay for everything like their current benefits but at the very least you could cut their health insurance benefits down to a supplemental insurance coverage that would pay whatever Medicare doesn't. This would drastically cut the cost of labor and the cost of our cars. And what happens then? Savings to the American people. Then the people buy more cars, thus creating more jobs, which means more spending, and even more taxes flowing into the government.

Like I said earlier these incentives will grow into more jobs for Americans, more spending in America, and that means more taxes coming in to offset the tax incentives given out. The government needs to start giving these incentives to our companies as soon as yesterday to start making this country work again.

That brings us to...

OUR GOVERNMENT

Our government? Where do I start with this one? Our government was made over 200 years ago for the betterment of us all as a nation. Today on the other hand our government is working for themselves with their own agendas. No longer does the politician want or for that matter need to help the people he is supposed to be representing. All he needs to do is show up occasionally and do whatever he feels like with his vote (or should I say our vote?) The people we elect are supposed to be working for us. But do they?

In President Obama's inauguration speech he stated that the American people are asking is our government too big? Is our government too small? Does our government work? He stated that he will show us it does indeed work. Well, Mr. President I think it does now!! (I know, I know, I just got done telling you that our government needs to do a lot of things different, just keep reading and you will understand what I am talking about.) Our government works right now as it is. The problem is it works for the wrong people. It doesn't work for the middle to lower classes. It works for the rich, the powerful, the people who have the loudest voice because they can "donate"

(donate=bribe)the most money to the parties or "donate" money to the respective government officials re-election campaign fund. So, yes our government does work. It is the best government money can buy!! The saddest part of all this is that it is perfectly legal. Our government officials are so worried about keeping their jobs that they will do whatever it takes just so they can keep doing what they are doing. I firmly believe they would sell their souls if they had to. This reminds me of the Eddie Murphy movie ***THE DISTINGUISHED GENTLEMAN.*** If anyone remembers the meetings he had in that movie, it didn't matter which way he went on the issues, he had money coming in from different backers to his campaign fund. I firmly believe this is how it works in our government. Put a senator in front of a lobbyist and that lobbyist says they will hold a benefit for his future campaigns if he votes for his particular lobby I would say that senator would vote the way the lobbyist asks him to. I can't blame that lobbyist. He is doing his job. I blame our government system where all our elected officials care about is how they can keep their job and that means they need money for advertising for their campaign and the lobbyists are providing it.

I will put it in real terms. When it comes to us as a people voting for our congressmen and senators who do we vote for? We vote for the person we believe will best suit our wants and needs, right? How do we know which one of those people agree with our feelings about issues that pertain to those wants and needs? The answer to that is we read the candidates propaganda, we watch the candidates commercials, we listen to the candidates radio commercials, and we read the papers. Where do you think the money comes from for all those posters, TV ads, radio ads, and newspaper ads? Yes, some of that money comes from people that truly donate money to the person they believe in, but most of the money comes from businesses, CEO'S, and rich people that want "their" man in office so they can control them to do what is best for them. Not what is best for the people that are his true constituents. The real people that all of his decisions will affect. Yes businesses in each state need a man that they can count on to help them out too. I am not saying that they don't. I am saying that people as a whole should be considered equal to the rich and the powerful businesses and the rich and powerful people that can give more money than the average family can.

Everybody (who the hell is this everybody that people talk about? Is everybody you and me. Or is it them and us? What is the real definition of everybody? OK, sorry got off on a tangent there...LOL!)says if things don't go the way you want from the person that was elected you can always vote him out. VOTE HIM OUT? Are you kidding me? Most of the time when a person gets elected to office you find out he is a shit head way before it is election time again, so you would want him out sooner than election time. For example, I live in Illinois, the land of Lincoln. This is the state where the governor not only gets license plates issued he usually is the person that actually makes them from the prison he is in. Our state is just impeached Rod "helmet hair" Blagojevich for trying to sell Barack Obama's vacated senate seat to the highest bidder. To quote old helmet hair's taped phone conversation "What I have here is gold. I am not just going to give it away for nothing". This is what I mean by our government is the best money can buy!!

I am a finance manager for a car dealership (like I said earlier) and I have heard of the same thing happening in my industry. I heard of a sales manager that was giving customers to his salespeople but he would then tell the salesperson that he (the sales manager) would get half the commission. So, if that sales person made 200 dollars for selling that car, he would have to give 100 dollars to his boss. If that sales person didn't give that manager his half he would not get anymore customers from that sales manager. So of courses the salespeople would give up half of their commission because half was better than nothing.

That is what is going on in our government, that is what is going on in our businesses, and that is what is going to keep going on until something is done about it.

So now you are thinking the same thing I am. How do we fix it? How do we fix the corruption in our government? What can our government do to help the American people out? Aren't you glad I am here to answer these questions?

The first thing our government needs to do to is realize that they are elected officials that are supposed to be working for their respective constituents and should do what is best for us not what is best for themselves and their own re-election. We as a people need to help this happen. (Again here is a sacrifice we need to make for the better good) We need to make our politicians be accountable. When they mess up (and they will) we need to speak out. We need to write them letters. We need to write letters to the newspapers, TV stations, we need to speak out to whomever we can whenever we can. Our power as a people is in our numbers. You might be saying "this is not the government policing the situation it is the people doing all the work." You are half right. You didn't let me finish. Once this is all done by the people the government needs to step in. Every state has 2 senators, that is how we are all equally represented in our government. God willing both senators are not corrupt in this situation. Lets assume they are not everybody here remembers peer pressure, right? Picture this...99 other senators pressuring the crooked senator into stepping down. (Blue by the way...that is the color of the sky in my world.) I know that this is not going to happen, but hey, it's a good thought right?

OK, back to reality now. What we need is a true law in place that would severely punish crooked politicians that break the law and abuse their powers. There also needs to be a law that polices the amount of money that can be collected from companies and individuals for campaign purposes. There is no reason why these candidates need to be collecting the amount of money they are collecting. There should also be a cap on how much money they can collect overall. Once this cap is hit the remaining money is donated to the community, city, or state that the person is running in. This puts the candidates on an even playing field. This makes everything equal. The election shouldn't be determined by who is willing to sell his votes to the highest bidders. Elections should be won on principles and where they stand. Not by who can raise the most money and by the most commercial air time. This commercial "salary" cap will also help communities all around our great nation with the excess money collected. If you actually set and keep a limit on money that is allowed to be used our communities would thrive from the overage. Not to mention it would not just be a popularity contest in elections. Instead of spending millions upon millions running the same commercials over and over again. I think the messages would be more powerful because they would be condensed and straight to the point.

Campaign spending reform can also contribute some money to this economy and to our communities as well. In the 2008 election featuring Barack Obama and John McCain they were allowed to raise all the money that they wanted and all the money they possibly could. Barack Obama did it the right way. (Yes, I still think he raised too much money) He opted to raise his money through small individual donations from individuals not the big lobbyists and political action committees.

In a speech at Roosevelt Middle School in Cedar Rapids, Iowa, Obama stated, "And as a candidate for President, I've tried to lead by example, and I've decided to run this race by turning down all contributions from federal lobbyists and the political action committees that the special interests use to pass out campaign money."

From Obama's official website, it showed-- before it was removed: "Obama supports public financing of campaigns combined with free television and radio time as a way to reduce the influence of moneyed special interests."

And get this...Barack Obama turned down the money from the presidential campaign financing fund. That is the fund that we all can give to when we file our taxes. If you check the box on your tax return if you choose to donate 3 dollars to this fund. The funny thing here is that doesn't decrease your tax return or increase your taxes owed for the year the donation is made. Where does it come from then? I think that is a fair question. It obviously comes from the taxes collected but it doesn't come from our own individual pockets. But we still pay for it another way. How about we put a thing on our tax forms that says donate 3 dollars to your local schools? Or donate 3 dollars to your local police department. Or even donate 3 dollars to the local salvation army. Just to let you know John McCain took over 84 million dollars from this fund. I am not saying it was wrong to do. That is what the money is there for. I just believe that setting money aside to elect a president is a load of crap considering how much money they raise on their own anyway.

I am a realist and I know that if it weren't for TV and advertising we wouldn't even know who was running or what they stand for. I am a person that watches too much television (just like most Americans do) and during elections you see commercial after commercial for all the candidates running. They all say they are for this and this is why. Or they are against this and this is why. Do I think this is necessary to determine who I would vote for? A resounding YES!! However, what we do need more of is actual debates. We need to see the people we are voting into office actually asked real questions submitted by the people that are going to be voting for them. I see debates with predetermined questions. I scream shenanigans!! It isn't too hard to answer a question that you are prepared for. I want the candidates to walk in and have the debate run by a mediator that pulls out the questions from a giant bucket with the persons name on it that wrote it so that person can stand up and be addressed like the question and answer mean something to the candidates. Is this too much to ask? I don't think so!!

Here is another movie reference for you. The movie is **MAN OF THE YEAR** starring Robin Williams. The man ran an election the way it should be run driving across country in a bus and **SPEAKING THE TRUTH!!!!** I also remember the debate he was in with the other two candidates, where he pointed out all the wrong doings his opponents were doing and how they contradicted what they had previously stated during the election process. I firmly believe that if a man ran an election based on truth and forthcoming information he would win by a landslide. I know I would rather vote for a man that has gone through true life situations like I have gone through. I would rather vote for a man that has filed for bankruptcy and come back from it than a man that was born with a silver spoon in his mouth and raised to be an elected official. I would rather vote for a man that has been run through the ringer in a divorce than has a political wife that stays with him just for the political view of it. I would rather vote for a man that has only a high school education and worked his way into his positions in life rather than having it handed to him on a silver platter by his father (can you say George W. Bush?) I would rather vote for a man that isn't afraid of speaking up for himself and others rather than saying what he thinks we want to hear. I would rather vote for a man who speaks to me like an equal not an inferior person to him. Is there a man or woman in this country like this?

I think that is enough about elections, don't you? It is time to get on to once the people are in office. We desperately need to do things differently for us to thrive in these hard times.

Taxes are a necessity to fund our military, to take care of people in this country that can no longer take care of themselves, or were never able to take care of themselves for that matter. I think it is time to institute a floating flat tax percentage. Floating by means of how much money you make at your job. The more you make the more you pay in taxes. The way our system works right now the people that can afford tax attorney's find every possible loop hole there is so they only have to pay the bare minimum in taxes while average American people pay whatever their accountant or tax preparer tells them to pay. My point is that the rich have everything at their disposal. Even if the rich get audited they have the money to pay attorney's to fight for them. The average American can not afford take the chances that the rich American people can. By going to a flat tax based on true income there would be no audits. There would be no need for the IRS. (I know I am contradicting myself by eliminating those jobs but what can I say I hate the IRS...LOL) Honestly this tax system we have in place is a true joke. I remember the movie (told you I quote and reference movies a lot) **THE FIRM** starring Tom Cruise where he was a tax attorney and they stated something like one of his clients is paying less than 5% income tax and he was still complaining. That is exactly how it shouldn't be. Everybody in this country should be treated equally especially when it comes to taxes.

Speaking of taxes I have an interesting story to tell you. As I told you earlier I work for a car dealer. I am a finance manager. I do state and local paperwork. I also get loans approved for people that need loans to buy their car. I actually figured something out. On average we sell 200 cars per month. The average sales tax for each transaction is between 900 and 1400 per transaction. Lets take a small average of just 1000 per transaction. That means in most months the dealership I work for generates 200,000 dollars of sales tax revenue for the state!! yes almost one quarter of a million dollars per month or 2.4 million dollars per year. We are but one dealership of many thousands across my state. Lets use a some round numbers here. Lets say there are roughly 2000 (I know there are more than that in Illinois alone) dealerships in Illinois. And each one of those dealerships does the same 200 cars per month. (I also know of some of those dealerships that do two to three times as many as that or more but once again I am saying as an average.) That gives the state of Illinois 4.8 billion dollars a year in sales tax revenue...and that is just from car dealerships (I use them as my basis because I have worked in dealerships for over 15 years). That doesn't take into account sales tax from department stores, gasoline stations, grocery stores, or just about any other retailer there is. (I am sure you don't want me to name them all here) How much actual sales tax money do you think there is in just Illinois? 15 billion? 25 billion? I don't think we will ever know. I am not even getting into the lottery money here. That would just take forever.. Holy crap I almost forgot one other thing. The river boat casino's. How much more money do these little cash cows bring into the state of Illinois (or any other states that have legalized gambling boats or casino's? So anywho my question is this....WHERE THE HELL IS ALL THAT MONEY GOING? I think we need to do an audit of our government.

If there is that much money involved on the state level how much is involved on a national level? (oh crap...my head hurts, what does an aneurysm feel like?) There are way too many hands in the cookie jar so to speak!! Where are the people that are going to audit the governments? Why haven't we heard about where all of our money goes? I know one thing for sure it doesn't all go into our school systems, our roads, or our overall well being as a community, city, state, or even nation.

Schools are the biggest concern for me. This is how our children are going to learn our history, simple math, English, (yes I believe English is still the language of this country and should be taught to all no matter where you come from. You want to live here you learn the language of the land...period.) and basic skills to survive in our world. Yet there are more cuts in our school systems than any other public funded program. (not a known fact just my opinion) Why is that? How come every time that the teachers need a raise there has to be a vote to raise taxes to pay them more money. Basically the government is asking the people who pay taxes if they want to pay more in taxes so the teachers can make more money and in turn pay more taxes too. Now how come whenever congress needs a raise the only people that have to vote on it is congress themselves? Where is my vote to say hell no to them getting a bigger piece of my tax money so they can mess up even more? I think I would vote to give me a raise every time I had a chance to also!! Who the hell wouldn't? If you just said "I wouldn't" to that statement you are full of shit plain and simple!!!!

Many years ago a young man was drafted first overall in the NFL. He signed an 11 million dollar contract and said it was great but it was not fair. And he didn't say that for the reason you would think. This young man was raised by his father who happened to be a teacher. He said that it was unfair because he was going to get paid more money than his dad will ever see in his lifetime being a teacher. He also said that teachers are the lowest paid most unappreciated people in this country. I have to agree with him!!

Here we are paying people (the president, the senators, the house of representatives, the governors, and the mayors) to lose our money, steal our money, and have nothing to show for our benefit. (sounds like the CEO's I spoke of earlier doesn't it?) I know I am not the only person here that is feeling like I am (or should I say we are) getting shafted.

Everyone here want to know how MESSED UP our elected officials are? Here is a very simple thing I am sure people didn't know. Our elected congressmen are requested (requested, not required) to vote when bills come up for a vote. Now here is the interesting part. They can vote yay, nay, or PRESENT. Yes our elected officials don't have to agree or disagree with a bill. They can literally say that yes they are here but we don't care if this bill passes or not. So they don't have to show up but if they do they can vote to not vote. Oh man I want that job. Show up when you can. Vote for only the stuff you feel like and collect your check. Why does this happen? Why are the people we elect to office not supporting our beliefs? Our elected officials should be required to be at every vote and they have to vote yay or nay based on what they feel is right. That is what we elected them for. We elected them to be our voice. We did not elect them to just sit on their asses and do nothing.

During the voting process in the House of Representatives or Senate our elected officials are supposed to be voting based on what the community they represent feels. Our elected officials do not do that. They vote on their own personal agendas and they also vote to help the businesses that put money in their pockets.

The question has been asked "Is our government too big? Or is it too small? Or is it just right?" Well Goldie locks I think it is just right. We do have the principles in place that make our checks and balances system the best throughout the entire world. I will repeat that, we have the "principles" in place to make our checks and balances system the best throughout the entire world. What we don't have in place is accountability and the actual checks and balances being followed as they were intended to be followed when they were written over 200 years ago by our founding fathers. Do you think George Washington was wondering what was in it for him if he passed a law? "Gee wiz, Martha if I pass this law to help the other Americans I get nothing for it. Nobody gave me any money to do it so I guess I won't!" You would have never heard him say that. Do you think Abraham Lincoln was sitting in front of his fireplace with his stovepipe hat on saying how much money he was going to get from the local blacksmith for his campaign, and if he didn't get enough he wouldn't care about what the blacksmith wanted? I highly doubt that was the case!! All they cared about was what was best for our country as a whole. What would help us grow as a nation. Help us all truly live life in the pursuit of true happiness.

When I played baseball as a little kid I was told many times to get back to basics. Remember what got you to the position you are in and keep doing that. That is what our government needs to do. Get back to the basics of what made this country the best country in the world!! Start being accountable for all actions. Start using the money wisely and not spending 20,000 dollars on a hammer and 30,000 dollars on a toilet seat. Start actually caring about this country and all the people in it and not just yourselves or the millions in donations you might lose if you act with a conscience. I am sure when you show the people who voted for you why they voted for you all will fall into place. We as a nation want our leaders to lead us into prosperity, happiness, and have an overall good feeling about being safe, both financially and physically. You want to keep your job start showing us why you deserve it. Start showing us how we are better off with you in there as opposed to another guy.

There is something to be said for new blood in power positions. Lets take the NFL for instance. This year (2009) we have 2 coaches that lead their teams to the Superbowl. Both of these coaches were never head coaches in the NFL before. They were not retreads like so many other coaches in the league. They had fresh minds, fresh ideas, and they were full of spunk. These 2 coaches have been head coaches only 2 years each. In 2 years they lead teams to the promised lands in their sport. In 2 years they reached the top and should stay there for awhile. One of these teams has never ever been to the Superbowl before. Why were these 2 guys able to do that? Because they worked together with the people underneath them. They worked together with the people over them. They didn't come in and say this is how we are going to do it. It is my way or the highway (although sometimes that is necessary). No, they came in with a team first attitude and the people underneath them bought what they were selling because they believed in what was being presented to them.

More proof our government is MESSED UP is that Senator Ted Kennedy's wife is asking for his supporters to donate money to his political action committee. She says by donating to his committee you will be helping him in his quest to establish health care for all Americans. "He believes that every American has the right to decent, quality, affordable health care, and fighting for that right is the cause of his life," Victoria Reggie Kennedy writes in the e-mail sent by her husband's Committee for a Democratic Majority.

Whoa!!! Let me get this straight. Senator Ted Kennedy needs my money to help him get health care for all Americans? As you will read later in this book I am for health care for all Americans but how does us donating money directly to his political action committee help with that? According to good old Wikipedia.com a leadership political action committee is defined like this: *A leadership PAC in U.S. politics is a political action committee that can be established by a member of Congress* *to support other candidates. The funds cannot be spent to directly support the owner of the PAC's own campaign (such as mail or ads), but may fund travel and make contributions to other campaigns. During the 2006 election cycle, 256 leadership PACs contributed over $37 million to federal candidates.*

Mrs. Kennedy is asking all of us to fund her husbands traveling and contributions to other members of congress. Umm, I may be mistaken here but I think that means bribe other members of congress. So if I give Mr. Kennedy 1000 dollars he takes that money and that money pays for him to travel to a location to meet with another member of congress. At this meeting he will then take money from his political action committee and give it to this congressman's political action committee so that congressman can go travel to meet with another congressman and talk about his agenda. To me this sounds an awful lot like bribing or paying off the congressman so they can get whatever they want.

If I donate money to Mr. Kennedy to help with health care in America how do I know that is what he is truly using my bribe money for? Oops, I mean donation? To me this sounds like the old telavangelists that used to be on TV. They would ask you for money to help support their church and their cause but they were really pocketing the money and using it for themselves. Lets say that we all send money to Mr. Kennedy's political action committee and he has to resign for health reasons, (he does have brain cancer you know and had a seizure at one of President Obama's inaugural balls) what happens to that money? Does he get to keep that money? Or does he give it to the person that is going to take over for him? If it stays in the PAC and someone else takes over that didn't agree with Mr. Kennedy's beliefs that means my money may go against what I believe.

Here are some examples of how this political action committee money has been spent in the past as per Wikipedia.com:

Rep. Richard Pombo has used his leadership political action committee to pay hotel bills ($22,896) and to buy baseball tickets ($320) for donors.

Rep. John Doolittle's leadership political action committee, <u>Superior California Federal Leadership Fund</u>, pays his wife's single-person company, Sierra Dominion Financial Solutions, 15 percent of all money raised ($68,630 in 2003-2004, $224,000 in 2005-2006). A campaign committee report in February said Doolittle's campaign still owed Julie Doolittle $137,000. The political action committee also has purchased $2,139 in gifts for Bose Corporation.

That is just 2 instances of politicians taking money donated to them to help the cause they are fighting for and using that money for their own personal gain. If there are these 2 that we know about what about the ones we don't know about? I wonder how much money is actually sitting in Mr. Kennedy's political action committee accounts? I am sure I am not sending any money to any of the politician's political action committees, ever, ever, freaking ever. The Chicago Cubs will win the World Series before they receive any of my money!! That means they will never see any of my money...lol!! (die hard Chicago Whitesox fan right here and if I can rip a Cubs fan any time I will)

Here is even more proof of how MESSED UP our government is. On February 6, 2009 our congressmen passed a 780 billion dollar economic stimulus package. This stimulus package started out as a 900 billion dollar stimulus package but it got some cuts. Of those cuts that were made the biggest ones that I see are from education and health care. Yep education and health care. Two of our most important things in this country. 16.5 billion dollars got cut for school construction, 3.5 billion dollars for higher education construction, 1 billion dollars for head start/early start, 98 million dollars for school nutrition, 2 billion dollars for HIT (Health Information Technology) grants, and 5.8 billion dollars for health prevention activity. That is almost 30 billion of the 120 billion that was cut. Why on earth are we cutting some of the most important things in this country? Like I said before there isn't enough money in it for the politicians and their lobbyists is why. I think they should have cut some of our foreign funding before they cut our own educational funding out of a stimulus package that was designed to stimulate our economy.

Right now I don't believe in my government because even though I have a say in who works for it I don't have a say in how things are done once that person gets in there. I am not a member of a team. I am a pawn in the game of life. You want to show us that our government works? You want us to believe you have our best interests at heart? Then show us that!! Do what you know is right even though it wouldn't be the popular thing amongst your peers. Show us that our government is (to quote Abraham Lincoln from the Gettysburg Address) "a government of the people, by the people, and for the people!!" And not one nation under the dollar with liberty and justice for none!! (except the rich and powerful that is, they get all they justice and liberties they want!)

When is our government going to realize that what is best for them is not best for the people of the United States? Shouldn't our government care more about our people than people that live in other countries?

Our government is truly MESSED UP!!

And that brings us to...

FOREIGN POLICIES

I just rambled on quite a bit about our government as it pertained to us here in the United States of America. But what about how our government deals with foreign countries? Does anyone out there know my answer? If you were paying attention at any point in this book you would know my answer. My answer/philosophy is SCREW EM!! I do not care about the other countries problems as long as we have our own problems. Our foreign policy should be wait until we fix our problems, and if we can help you we will, but not before.

The officially stated goals of the foreign policy of the United States, as mentioned in the Foreign Policy Agenda of the U.S. Department of State, are "to create a more secure, democratic, and prosperous world for the benefit of the American people and the international community." I will try to point out in this chapter that what we are doing in other countries doesn't benefit this country one bit. With the exception of our direct neighbors, Canada and Mexico that is. Even they are more like a 70/30 split where we give 70% and get back

30% from them. But hey it is better than what the rest of the world gives back to us.

My first priority is *this* country and all the people in it. We have allies when it is convenient for the allies not when it is necessary for us and our well being. The United Nations can get bent for all I care too. It seems like we are the only country actually following there rules. (Excluding George W. and his I don't care what they say lets go to war anyway attitude)

If I were in charge of foreign policies it would be really really simple. **SCREW EM**!!! (by the way screw em was going to be the original name of this book but I thought messed up looked better...see even I have to be politically correct every now and then.) I would pull all of my troops out of every country (but keep them at my bases and embassy's just in case). I would put heavy taxes on products imported into our country unless it was 50/50 or better to our exports to that country. I would cut food assistance to other countries. I would cut all financial aid to other countries. I would stop importing oil from OPEC unless they lowered the price to us and accepted some of our goods to even it out.

The **SCREW EM** foreign policy explained in detail...

You want something from us we get something in return. Iraq you want our help to keep democracy there. In exchange we get oil for free. The current war in Iraq is costing the United States 12 billion dollars a month (not to mention American soldiers lives which are worth more than any amount of money or oil you could ever give). What are we getting out of it? Absolutely nothing is what we are getting out of it. So every month from now on we get 12 billion dollars of oil. Don't like it? Well SCREW YOU, we are out of there.

Japan you want your products in the United States? Then you have to take equal amounts of our products there. I don't have the exact number of cars we import from Japan to here but I do know that it is way more than the number of American cars Japan imports. You want us to continue to buy Japanese cars here? Better start buying more American cars there!! 50/50 or better remember. OK, as a realist I know that might not be possible. So here is the alternative. Build more factories here so Americans can contribute to the manufacturing of the products. If this is not acceptable then we tax your cars until your prices are equal or greater than ours. Either way my country is going to get some money from you doing business here!! Cars are just the beginning of what Japan has imported here. They have almost all of our technology(stereos, TV's, computers, etc) sales here. Why you might be asking? Because my dear reader they build it cheaper over there because the Japanese government doesn't have minimum wages over there. They don't have the benefits that our employees have here. They can literally work a person to the bone and pay them very little. So because of that they build them well but inexpensively in Japan which makes their products more appealing to us the American consumer because we truly are looking for the best value for our dollar. So I say foreign product tax it is. If Japan's products were equally priced to an American product I would say that most if not all of us would buy American first. Once this tax is in place the money would go back into our government and lower our income and sales taxes.

Here is an example. If you saw an American made surround sound system in the best buy that costs 250 dollars and a Japanese surround sound system of equal quality and equal features and benefits but costs 50 dollars less you would buy the Japanese product every time, we all would. Now picture same surround sound system from America at 250 dollars and the same Japanese product at 250 dollars (the extra 50 dollars to our new foreign products tax) which would you buy? Twenty years ago I would have almost guaranteed you still would have said the Japanese one, because American products were shabby products at best. But in the year 2009 I can honestly say I believe American products to be equal if not slightly better than Japanese products. So today I would say we buy the American made product over the Japanese product. How long do you think Japan would be able to keep up with that tax hitting them every time? Not long at all. This would cause their products quality to slip as they cut costs and soon the people that would buy Japanese no matter what would come back to American because of the quality. And lets not forget one other factor in this. With Japan's cost cutting and subsequently the quality dropping more Japanese and other countries would want American products because of their quality over Japan. Thus creating more jobs here in the good old U.S. of A!! That sounds like a win-win-win situation for us here!!

Let's say that Japan wants to still keep business here in the United States and agrees to build factories over here and use our workers. Once again a win-win situation for us because now our workers get jobs and we get taxes from that and from the Japanese companies factories we get even more taxes. There is a downside to that. The profit would still go to Japan and not stay here. Well, we can't win them all I guess. But two thirds of the money still stays here and that is better than the 50/50 rule.

Now a lot of people are probably thinking "you can't do that. You can't just not help people in need." You are right we can't just not help people. However, how about we help the people here in our country first. We have a homeless problem here and we have a 8.1% unemployed rate here in America (as of February 6th 2009). We have people here that need our help too. What are we doing about these people? Are you saying we should put other countries people before our own? How many commercials have you seen where they are talking about pennies a day will help feed these kids over in some third world country? How do we know that money is getting to these people. How do we know that there are people with their hand in the cookie jar there just like there is here? I mean come on. We are at least semi regulated here. Do you really think these countries are not skimming off the top? Or for that matter holding out and keeping food and money away from these people.

I totally believe that the government and armies of these third world countries keep the food and funding away from these people just to keep them down. Another example of the man keeping them down. (Sorry, I couldn't resist that) I'll give you the perfect example of governments getting rich and the poor people suffering because of it.

Saddam Hussein had palace after palace with gold toilets, artwork, and fancy cars. Yet his people were living in huts and caves. Is this right? I do believe that this is happening more than not in these countries. The rich truly do get rich off the poor in these countries. At least here we get the courtesy of being lied to about it!! There they get told straight out that they are getting screwed out of their house, money, and sometimes their lives. Do I think it is right that this is happening? No I do not. But I don't put these people ahead of the American people.

Our foreign aid policy needs to be taken away completely. We are giving financial aid to Sub-Saharan Africa; Asia and the Near East, Latin America and the Caribbean, Europe, and Eurasia. This aid is given for the following reasons: Economic Growth, Agriculture and Trade; Democracy, Conflict, and Humanitarian Assistance. I am speaking as an American citizen here when I say this. Who gives a shit about any of this stuff? I know I don't!!

The amount of money set aside from our taxes to do this for the fiscal year 2009 was 39.5 billion dollars. What do you think we can do in America with 39.5 billion dollars? I know, more bow and arrow research. (Dang, I crack myself up sometimes.) I am about to show you what our government is going to do with this money: (compliments of Wikipedia)

- *$2.4 billion to improve responsiveness to humanitarian crises, including food emergencies and disasters, and the needs of refugees*
- *$938 million to strengthen USAID's operational capacity*

- *$2.3 billion to help Iraq, Afghanistan, Pakistan and West Bank/Gaza achieve economic, democratic, security and political stabilization and to advance their overall development*

- *$2.1 billion for State Department and USAID programs in Africa to address non-HIV/AIDS health, economic growth and democratic governance needs and to help promote stability in Sudan, Liberia, Zimbabwe and Somalia in support of the President's 2005 commitment to double aid to Africa by 2010*

- *$4.8 billion for the Global HIV/AIDS Initiative, which directly supports the first year of the President's new five-year, $30 billion plan to treat 2.5 million people, prevent 12 million new infections, and care for 12 million afflicted people*

- *$550 million to support the Mérida Initiative to combat the threats of drug trafficking, transnational crime, and terrorism in Mexico and Central America*

- *$1.7 billion to promote democracy around the world, including support for the President's Freedom Agenda*

- *$385 million to support the President's Malaria Initiative to reduce malaria-related deaths by 50 percent in 15 target African countries by 2010*

- *$94 million for the President's International Education Initiative to provide an additional 4 million students with access to quality basic education through 2012*

- *$64 million for the State Department and USAID to support the President's Climate Change Initiative to promote the adoption of clean energy technology, help countries adapt to climate change, and encourage sustainable forest management*

- *$4.8 billion for foreign military financing to the Middle East, Latin America, Europe and Eurasia, including $2.6 billion for Israel*

- *$2.2 billion for the Millennium Challenge Corporation to improve agricultural productivity, modernize infrastructure, expand private land ownership, improve health systems, and improve access to credit for small business and farmers*

There are a total of 3 things on that list that I agree with giving funding to. The 4.8 billion dollars given for the Global HIV/AIDS initiative, the 550 million dollars to combat the threats of drug trafficking, transnational crime and terrorism in Mexico and Central America, and the 385 million to support the Malaria Initiative. I agree with these things for only one reason. They could have a direct affect on me and my country. HIV/AIDS initiative and the Malaria Initiative could affect us all health wise. And the drug trafficking does affect us all.

Our government is spending 2.4 billion dollars to improve responsiveness to humanitarian crises, including food emergencies and disasters, and the needs of refugees. What about America's food emergencies? What are we doing to help the people here? I mean come on. To quote the great movie of *LIVE FREE OR DIE HARD* it took FEMA 5 days to get water to the Superdome (in New Orleans after Katrina hit.) What have we done to improve our own disaster responsiveness? This money gets cut out completely...NEXT!!!

938 million dollars to strengthen the USAID's operational capacity? What the hell does that mean? Does it mean more jobs for politician's brother-in-laws? I am willing to bet yes. So we are giving 938 million dollars to strengthen the system that is giving away 39.5 billion. So we are spending money from a program to make that very program stronger. (There is that headache again...go away damn you!!) This money gets cut out completely... NEXT!!

Here is the one that gets my goat a lot. 2.3 billion dollars to help Iraq, Afghanistan, Pakistan and West Bank/Gaza achieve economic, democratic, security and political stabilization and to advance their overall development. So we are spending 2.3 billion dollars to help other countries economies. Who gives a shit about those countries economies? I can't remember the last time I read an article where those countries gave money back to the U.S. Because they are so stable now that they don't need our help. Oh, wait, they are not stable! They are not doing anything but fighting each other. We are trying to bring democracy to Iraq, Afghanistan, Pakistan, and West Bank/Gaza. These are the same people I see burning American flags in the streets. These are the same people throwing rocks at our soldiers that are trying to "help" them. They want our money but they would kill us in a split second if they could. SCREW EM!! Put this money back here in America where most of our people would appreciate it. This money gets cut out completely... NEXT!!

We give 2.1 billion dollars for State Department and USAID programs in Africa to address non-HIV/AIDS health, economic growth and democratic governance needs. This money is also used to promote stability in Sudan, Liberia, Zimbabwe and Somalia. If it isn't AIDS I don't care about it. (Until it poses a threat to us, I never will care about it either.) Once again we are giving billions of dollars to promote economic growth to a country other than ours. As for promoting stability to those countries, I say this: Let them fight it out. Whoever wins the war we can work out some solid trade agreements and make some money and stabilize our economies together. I know I should not being saying for them to fight it out. It isn't politically correct and as a human it should never be OK to promote a war, but hey lets face it. If we keep giving money to these countries trying to "stabilize" the region, what do you think they are they going to do with this money? I'll tell you what...they are going to buy more weapons and fight anyway. So I say don't give them anymore money and let the best country win with no help from us. (Here is an interesting point that was brought up by one of my African-American friends. We as Americans have fought many people in this world but we have never fought against a predominately black country like Africa. Just an interesting tidbit I thought I would share with you all.) This money gets cut out completely...NEXT!!

We have dedicated 1.7 billion dollars to promote democracy around the world. Who cares if there is democracy anywhere but here? Most Americans don't care of some little rinky dink country has a president or a dictator as their leader. As a matter of fact I am willing to bet that most Americans couldn't tell you 10 countries that have dictators and 10 that have democracies. Do you want to know why? Because we DON'T CARE!! That's why. So lets put that 1.7 billion dollars back to the American people...NEXT!! (like I said earlier harsh times call for harsh measures.)

To tell you all the truth this next one I am on the fence about. 94 million dollars for the President's International Education Initiative. I think education is important no matter what. But at the same time I think it is the responsibility of the government of that particular country's not ours. So I still say put that 94 million toward the education of our own children in this country and I won't say screw em here because it is not the kids fault as to where they were born. I just feel bad for the kids in these countries, but I also feel bad for some kids here too, and our kids come first. A little side note here. I am pointing out billions upon billions of dollars spent for democracy and stabilization of regions but only 94 million for education of children. That just goes to show you what is more important in our governments eyes. Anyway back to the point this money goes back to us and not other countries, so...NEXT!!

64 million dollars to support the Climate Change Initiative. The question I have here is this: Is this money being spent in our country for our scientists to work on this initiative? If so I can be for this. If it is being spent in other countries to study climate change then to Hell with it and bring it back here so our guys can use the money. Another side note here. Once again billions upon billions on democracy and stabilization but only

64 million on global climate change. Priorities are all **MESSED UP** on this one.

When I read that we are sending 4.8 billion for foreign military financing to the Middle East, Latin America, Europe and Eurasia, and that included 2.6 billion to Israel, to say I was shocked and appalled by this would be an understatement. The Middle East military would kill us in the blink of an eye if they get the chance. Who is Latin America fighting anyway? Europe and Eurasia? Does that include France? If it does I say SCREW EM. Oh hell, I say SCREW EM all anyway. As for Israel, yes they are our "ally" but (to quote Janet Jackson here) what have they done for us lately? Not a damn thing. So that money gets cut out completely...NEXT!!

The last section of this 39.5 billion dollars is the 2.2 billion dollars that we set aside to improve agricultural productivity, modernize infrastructure, expand private land ownership, improve health systems and improve access to credit for small business and farmers. Now had I thought they were talking about people in our own country I would say that 2.2 billion dollars is just a drop in the bucket. But, I know they are not talking about America so I say it is way too much. Our government is trying to help other country's people own land when we are going to have over 5 million people lose their land in this country. Our government is giving money to foreign countries to improve their health systems when 45 million people in this country do not have health coverage and therefor can't get basic health care services provided for them. (More on this in my health care chapter later on in this book). And last, but not least, our government is giving money to other countries to improve access to credit for these people when our country is probably the largest credit crunch in decades. 2.2 billion dollars back to the American people it is.

All of these programs are funded from our tax dollars. All of these programs are designed to help other countries. Once again what about our country? What about our people here?

What I am trying to say in all of this is that I am sure our government can find much better ways to spend the money here rather than in other countries. I understand that we are the 7th richest country in the world and people look to us for help. (To quote the movie SWING VOTE yet again) If we are one of the richest countries in the world why is it so expensive for us to live here? The answer to that question is this - Because we give a lot of our own money away to other countries so they can try and live like us.

One other foreign policy that needs to be worked on is OPEC!! The Organization of the Petroleum Exporting Countries. These people have way to much power in our country. Every time that prices drop they cut production of oil to drive the prices up so they can make more money. It doesn't cost them any more to produce it, it just costs us more to buy it because they are shortening the supply.

I read an article recently stating that the government of Venezuela needs oil prices at or above 65 dollars per barrel for their economy to be stable. In that same article another of OPEC country needed oil to be over 35 dollars per barrel for their economy to be stable. ***SCREW EM!!*** What if our country came out and said we need oil to be at 30 dollars per barrel or our economy would fall apart. Would it matter to them? Hell no!! All they care about is their own economy. So we should too.

We can take control of what OPEC does all we have to do is cut them off for awhile. Wait, wait, wait, don't go into a panic about that just yet. Do we need their oil? Unfortunately, the answer there is yes but we can still cut them off, kinda!! First thing we do is buy all the oil we can store in this country from OPEC. (Now when I say we, I mean our government, not the individual oil companies in our country) This will drive the price down for a little while. So we keep buying and buying until our refineries are full, our storage facilities are full, and we make sure our reserves couldn't possibly hold any more oil. I mean we would be overflowing with oil at this point. After that is done we cut them off. We tell OPEC that we are not going to be buying any of their oil at all. They will not be allowed to sell their oil in our country at all. What we have will last us and what we use we can replenish by producing from our own oil sources. This is what I call a semi bluff.

What do you think they would do then? We are the biggest consumer of their oil. We buy their oil no matter what because we need it and they know we need it. Well now in their eyes we won't need it because we have the stockpile and our own sources to replenish that stockpile. If my theory is correct they will start asking us to be buyers again. They will start offering us better pricing, but that won't be enough for us. We need some guarantees from them. We need some signed contracts from them. We need a set minimum of oil provided by them no matter what. If they cut production it can not go down less than this minimum or they will be subject to extra taxes on their oil to offset the price that will be achieved because of the lack of supply.

As for the semi bluff here is why it is a semi bluff and not a full bluff or even a full all out cut off without worry. We can and do produce our own oil from our own American companies. These companies can not keep up with the production that is needed. But at the same time that we are cutting off OPEC we can work on our alternative fuel sources like ethanol and use it to offset some of the oil we lose from OPEC. If OPEC calls our bluff we start drilling in the Alaskan oil reserves that are not being touched. I am sure once we put the screws, so to speak, to OPEC they will cave. I mean come on, they are saying prices need to be at 65 dollars per barrel now and we are buying millions of barrels a day from them. What if we are buying none. Now that oil price has to skyrocket and other countries may take our side and start cutting off OPEC also and then OPEC will either do what is necessary to get all of our business back or they will be disbanded completely.

If you want to do business in America you need to follow our rules not yours. There is no way in Hell that a foreign entity like OPEC should have a strangle hold on our economy like this and we need to take that control back!! We are a super power in this world and yet OPEC controls us like we are some puppets in their show. So I say once again ***SCREW EM!!*** You do things our way here or **GTFO (*GET THE FUCK OUT*)** out of our country and our economy!!!

In an article I was reading for research on the Media chapter of this book I actually read something that belongs here. It says that our media is the only one in the whole world that reports as the good Samaritans that we are. Other media report America as greedy, arrogant, and self centered/only caring about the United Stares and no other countries or people. I say if this is truly how we are perceived in this world lets just go ahead and actually be that way. I am so sick and tired of doing nice things for other countries and not even get a thank you.

That reminds me of a television show that I saw recently. It was the **GEORGE LOPEZ SHOW**. On this particular episode he was distraught about his mother never ever thanking him for doing anything for her. He let her take a shower at his place for a few days because her shower drain was clogged at her house. Did he get a thank you? No!! All he got was grief about why he hasn't gone over to fix the drain. When he finally caves in and goes over there her whole bathroom is a pig sty. Cabinets falling off the hinges, tiles coming off in the shower, pretty much just a super nasty bathroom. George's wife convinces him that if he rebuilt her entire bathroom for her she would have to say thank you to him. She told him that this would be the biggest thing he ever did for his mom and that she would be really grateful and he would get his thank you. So he told his mom a pipe burst in her placed while he was working on it and she would have to stay at his house until he fixed it. 3 days later the bathroom was done and it looked great. He brought his mom back home had her close her eyes so he could surprise her with her new beautiful bathroom. She walked in looked around and said "that hook is way too high on the door, how am I supposed to reach that to hang my robe on it?" My first thought was you ungrateful bitch!! And then it was brought up on the show that the reason she didn't say thank you all those times is because she felt that because of what she did for him as a child, (raising him as a single parent, sacrificing her early adult life so he could have a home) that she deserved everything he gave her. And then I thought she was still an ungrateful bitch and it wasn't George's fault he was born at the time he was born. She should be grateful that he does stuff for her because he has a choice to do them or not. She had no choice because of her irresponsibility she was forced into the situation of having a son at a young age.

That is exactly how I feel about the other countries of this world. We do so much for them with no thank yous. No return on our money and time. These country's media report us as the bad guy. The country that only cares about themselves. And I think it is about time we do just that. It is time for us to put our people first.

It is time for America to flex its muscle and power over these other countries. You want to do business here you do it our way not your way. You want our help, we want something in return. If you can not give us something in return to heck with you, we don't need you anyway. We should not be scared of anyone or any country. We have the technology to patrol the world's military activities. If someone launches a squadron of jets against us we shoot down those planes and then bomb that airport. If they start to make a move on us at all we bomb the base it is coming from. These other countries should not be allowed to push us around at all. We need to take the control back. Right after he bombed the heck out of Iran, Ronald Reagan once said "he counted on America to be passive, he counted wrong!!" I say we replace the "he" in that quote with "they" and show the world that we will not just sit back and get told what to do anymore.

This is what I think of helping all these other countries...***SCREW EM!!*** Our foreign policies are truly... **MESSED UP!!.**

I watch CNN every now and then they talk about how the United States is doing wrong to this country or that country....who cares? I know I don't!! Once again ***SCREW EM!!***

And that brings us to ...

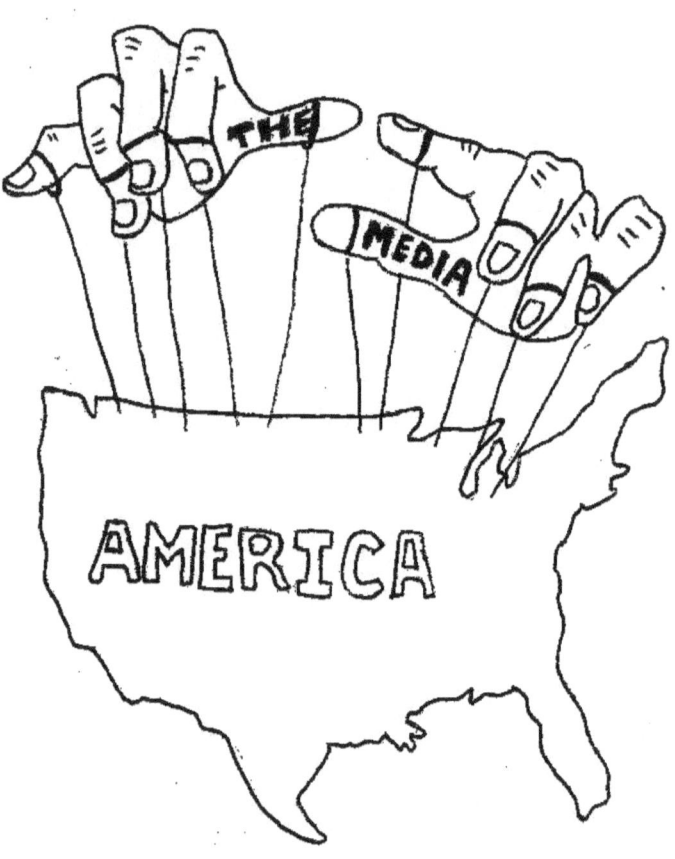

THE MEDIA

This might be the most insightful part of this book. I am a firm believer in the media being a great asset when used properly. However, in our beloved country it is a part of the problem, not the solution. As the picture above states I firmly believe that our media manipulates all of America. We are just the media's puppets and we are glad to be manipulated. Would you like me to explain my theory? Yes? I thought so!!

The media can make things happen just by saying that they will happen. Here is an example of that.

In the early 70's everything was in short supply, especially oil. When Americans heard the word shortage, they would jump out and purchase these things as quickly as possible. They would also stock up on these items so they wouldn't have to worry about running out of them. Nobody wanted to stand in line for anything. However, when it came to getting gas they had to wait in line. These people waited in lines that were sometimes over a mile long just to get a few gallons of gas. It was like the old food lines in Russia.

Did you know that in 1973 there was actually a toilet paper shortage in the United States. Yep you read it right a toilet paper shortage. On December 19, 1973 the writers of the Tonight Show, starring Johnny Carson, had heard earlier in the day that the federal government was falling behind in getting bids to supply toilet paper and that in a few months it could be possible that there would be a toilet paper shortage in the United States. They took this rumor and made a joke for Mr. Carson. That evening Johnny stood on the stage and said "you know what is disappearing off supermarket shelves? Toilet Paper!! There is an acute shortage of toilet paper in the United States."

Guess what happened? The next day the 20 million Americans that watched the show ran out and bought all the toilet paper they could carry. By noon on December 20, 1973, practically every store in America was completely out of stock!! Stores even tried rationing toilet paper to their customers. Even that didn't help them keep up with the demand. People kept coming and coming. They had to have their toilet paper. I mean if Johnny says it's true it must be true! Right?

A few days later Johnny went back on the air apologizing to his viewers. He explained it was all just a joke and that there really wasn't going to be a toilet paper shortage. But this did not help the situation. People kept right on buying it because they saw there store shelves still running out of the white gold. It actually took a total of 3 weeks to have the shelves restocked and the shortage was over.

What has this story taught us? It taught us that if the media says it, even if it isn't true, it will come true because people in our country believe everything that our media says. The media is run by corporations and the government. There are people in charge that decide what we see on TV, read in the newspapers and magazines, and hear on the radio. No kidding right? I am not just talking about what TV shows should be on the air . I am talking about what news stories should be aired and which ones shouldn't be aired.

This reminds me of a very good movie starring Robin Williams. ***GOOD MORNING VIETNAM*** is the movie. In this movie Robin plays an Air force radio "Shock" jock for armed forces radio during the Vietnam conflict. He was a great personality and a great boost to the moral of all the soldiers that listened to him. (I do believe it was based on a true story as well) Part of his characters duties was reading the news. In the movie the news would print out and 2 guys would sit there and cross out stories he was not allowed to read and circle the stories he was allowed to read. Anything that would bring the fighting men's morale down would get crossed out. Anything that would put the military system in a bad light would get crossed out. Only feel good stories would be allowed to be broadcast. He eventually got pulled off the air for reading one of the "bad" but true stories over the air. He was later reinstated only to be taken off permanently after the military found out one of his Vietnamese friends was actually supporting the other side.

I told you those stories to tell you this story.

About 3 years ago I couldn't log onto MSN, AOL, or YAHOO without reading how the housing markets bubble is going to burst some day. Every article said that the housing market was too good to be true. There is an article dated June 3, 2005 by Madeleine Brand where she interviewed a Yale professor named Robert Shiller and he said the housing market is a "bubble"--meaning prices are out of touch with economic reality-- and he predicts the market will collapse. The only question, he says, is when. Here are all of us living in America happy in our homes. Enjoying life, and not worrying about if our house was worth what we paid. We most certainly were not worried about owing more on our homes than what it was worth because housing values were continually going up. Our economy was still flourishing and people still had jobs. It was like a fairy tale. OK, maybe not all Americans but it was for some Americans anyway

Then the media decided things are going so great something must be wrong. There has to be a reason so many houses are being bought and sold in this country. There is no way these houses are worth what people are selling them for. What can we do to find out if we are right? Let's keep interviewing people that know something about the housing market until we find someone that will agree with this theory and let's blow it out of proportion. Is this the way it happened? Did our media really plot like this? I don't know but it sure seemed like it to me. Here we are living the American dream. Enjoying things as they were. Then somebody has to report bad news that may or may not happen.

Would the housing market bubble still have "burst"? I think it would have. But we could have maybe prevented so many people from losing their homes. I mean if so many people knew what was going on why didn't anyone step in and stop all the bad lending? Why didn't the government agencies that back home loans stop approving these so called bad mortgages? Had these steps been taken I don't believe it would have happened as fast as it did. And it most certainly wouldn't have affected as many people as it did. How about, if you know something is going to happen like this professor says he did, why not go to the people that can help solve it? Why not work with the people that could have helped the situation instead of talking to the media. If this one professor thought this I am sure other people in the know did as well. Why weren't things being done to prevent it from happening? My guess is because then the media wouldn't have the story they wanted.

I firmly believe that you get back what you put out. If all you put out is negativity, then that is all that is going to happen. If you put out positive things more positive things will come your way. If the media put out our economy is recovering I bet it would. I know I would love to flip stations and see reports on my local news station saying "Our economy is rebounding. Confidence is high in America once again. People are out buying cars and houses again." Here is the best part of that positive story. It is true. People are still buying houses, people are still buying cars, and confidence is high in America. I see people moving into houses still. I work for a car dealership and people still are buying cars. And confidence is a state of mind. One person may be confident in America and one person may not be. But because one person is confident it would be true. Do you think if that headline were printed, read on TV, and broadcast on the radio that it would come true? I am willing to bet that peoples moods would get better and happy people are buyers, happy people are investors, and happy people are just that, HAPPY! Things would turn around because people would believe it.

Today's journalists prefer to form public opinion rather than inform on it. They would much rather tell you what is right or wrong rather than letting you form your own opinion.

Our media likes to use scare tactics to get us to watch, listen, or read it. Have you ever watched TV and have a news break come on and tell you that they will tell you the rest of the story on the 11 o'clock news. If the story was strong enough to have a commercial for it just tell me what it is now. Imagine hearing this "tornadoes touching down near your area? Tune in at 11 for more information." Do you think you are having scare tactics used against you there?

Media omissions, distortion of truth, inaccuracy, and bias in the U.S. is something that people outside the USA realize more and more everyday. Because of these omissions, distortions, inaccuracy, and bias in the media today it is hard for the average American citizen to get an open and objective view of the real issues that involve our country. Most of the time, when I have a question I want to know the answer to, I have to look outside the mainstream media that we have here in America. I go on line and read as many different stories as I possibly can about the subject I am looking for. Then I try and find truth in these stories by looking at more stories about those stories. I know for a fact half of the stories I have read and even quoted in here most of you never heard of or read because they were put on the back burner.

Right here is where I am going to lose a lot of people because I have certain beliefs that are outside the mainstream media. For instance I firmly believe we did not have a man land on the moon. I believe it was all staged. I was able come to this conclusion by watching videos of the "moon landing" and by watching some videos that were not produced in this country. (These same video's can be found on the internet easily just type moon hoax in Google to find them.) If you watch them and compare the footage of the "real moon landing video" you will see that they are the same footage but these videos point out the mistakes made by the people staging the landing. After doing your own research on this you can form your own opinion. But I am sure you will agree after seeing both video's the one released by the government, and the one I am referring to you about the mistakes, you will agree with me.

The mainstream media here in the United States is under so much pressure to make a profit that they truly avoid controversial and sensitive issues that may either criticize our corporate America or upset their current readers, watchers, or listeners causing them to stop buying into their respective product. You want to start losing readers of a newspaper print something that the majority of the country doesn't agree with. You want to stop having people listen to your radio station have it publicly go against something that the public believes in. Let us not forget the TV market. The quickest way to lose people watching your station is to show something controversial. Proof of that was the boycott against a certain network when they decided to show a TV show where the actress came out of the closet as a lesbian. Or the time that a certain network aired the first ever bare butt on a prime time cop show. Remember how many people protested those shows? Remember how many times we heard about advertisers pulling out because of the controversial aspects of the show. And no advertising, no show.

Because of the mainstream media being so driven by sales profit and advertising dollars governments and businesses agendas are easier to push onto the people with a lot less criticism. And the more that happens over time, people will get used to the lower quality of media, and propaganda becomes easier to push on to the people.

An uninformed or falsely informed population means that more foreign policies can go without being noticed by our people. That is not to mention government policies being put into place for our own country. You just read above in the economy chapter how we are spending money from the TARP program for bow and arrow research. Was that publicized in the mainstream media? No it wasn't. I had to look and look hard on the internet to find it.

The United States government is increasing its secrecy. They are classifying more and more documents and using more propaganda and fear to scare the citizens here into giving up more of their civil rights so we can fight the war on terror. With the media being scared to present the truth for fear of upsetting us or upsetting the government we may never know all of the true things our government is doing or will do.

There is no formal censorship in the USA, but there is what some call "Market Censorship" — that is, mainstream media do not want to run stories that will offend their advertisers and owners. Because of this self imposed censorship, the media ends up censoring themselves and not reporting on many important issues, including corporate practices. Another thing about this self imposed censorship is that the media is more interested in attracting viewers and readers. Because of this the mainstream television stations report the same stories at the same time and objective reporting gets pushed to the side.

At a media conference in March 2007, Dan Rather stated some of his concerns regarding the state of journalism in the U.S. An article from *CNET* summarized some of Rather's key points: "So many journalists—there are notable exceptions—have adopted the go-along-to-get-along (attitude)," he said. So, because of this "access game," journalism has degenerated into a "very perilous state" This is what I am talking about. Even one of the most respected journalists of our time thinks that our media is too scared to report all that needs to be reported.

How can we as a country believe in our media when they don't even believe in themselves? Dan Rather even said "As media conglomerates get bigger, the gap between newsrooms and boardrooms grows, and the goal becomes satisfying shareholders, not citizens."

Is this truly what Americans deserve? The media is selling out to the highest bidder. The TV media is under pressure from their bosses and from the corporate sponsors to be entertaining rather than informing and because of that people are even more ignorant than ever. What happened to the journalists getting reliable sources and getting to the truth? What happened to freedom of the press? Isn't that part of the first amendment? Right now freedom of the press means that they are free to sell out to whomever they wish.

Speaking of good news, I would love to start an all good news channel. We can call it GNN. The Good News Network. Where we just report good news all the time. Who knows it might just work!! I bet it would get great ratings too!!

Here is proof that good news in our media influences our country. It happened February 24th, 2009. On this day The Federal Reserve Chairman Ben Bernanke told the world that he believes that the recession might end in 2009, with the recovery starting in 2010. He was very optimistic and upbeat when announcing this. Well guess what happened? This news got to Wall Street and because of the confidence that Mr. Bernanke exuded the Dow Jones Industrial Average went up 236 points. All of this because the man in charge of the money for our country said it is going to start getting better, maybe. Good news reported and good news happens in return. Now if he could just instill that confidence in every interview he does we might be out of this trouble sooner rather than later.

With that being said, one other aspect of the media I don't like is the all in all stupidity of it. I will give you yet another example of what I am talking about.

I just read an article about the Superbowl this year. In this article a certain "journalist" actually asked Larry Fitzgerald (arguably the best wide receiver in the NFL) "Larry, are you excited about being in this game?" Are you kidding me? Larry Fitzgerald, the man that has the record for the most yards in playoff history!! Larry Fitzgerald who plays for the Arizona Cardinals, the team that has never ever been to the Superbowl. (I'll repeat that...The Arizona Cardinals have never ever been to the Superbowl.) Larry Fitzgerald the former ball boy of the Minnesota Vikings. This guy still calls Chris Carter (former Wide Receiver of the Vikings) Godfather. All that information about Larry Fitzgerald out there and this moron actually asks a dumb question like that. Why didn't he just ask him how does it feel to breathe? Or even ask him...hey Larry, Now that you are making millions upon millions of dollars do you feel like you can finally get that car you always wanted? I can not believe the stupidity here!! I could come up with some great questions for him. For instance...Larry, you now hold the record for the most yards ever in the playoffs beating out Jerry Rice. Did Jerry call and congratulate you for this accomplishment? If he says yes I would ask what did Jerry say? If no my next question would be...do you feel like you are the best receiver in the game today? Or even...Is there any advice you can give to a young man playing pee wee football or even high school football that would help them try and beat your record in their future? (I am sure that would get some good laughs.)

Have you ever heard the term beating a dead horse? I am sure it was invented for the media. They continually jump on bandwagons and ride them to the end of the trail. But here is the thing - sometimes they do not know when to get off. It is like they get to the end of a roller coaster ride and scream "let's do it again". It is like when I tossed up my baby girl up at the age of 2 she wouldn't stop saying again daddy, again.

The analogy I am going to use here is the Terrell Owens story that seems to never end. (Yes, another sports analogy. I am a guy remember?) Terrell is a guy that is a good teammate in Dallas. His teammates like him, they respect him, and he is supportive of them. (By the way I am a die hard Dallas Cowboys fan) Case in point was a couple years ago when my beloved Cowboys were in the playoffs, the quarterback Tony Romo, fumbled a super slick ball (that was bullshit!! I am sure the Seahawks doctored that ball so it would slip out of Tony's hand. Did you see the picture of that ball. It looked like it was dipped in Vaseline!!) on a fieldgoal that would have given the Cowboys the lead. So instead of getting the lead they lost the game and the media jumped right on Tony and blamed him for the whole thing. The next day Terrell defended his QB and said that Tony is the unquestioned leader of this team and he supported him in every way. He also stated that it was a team loss and one play did not make the team lose.

Tony Romo then shut everyone out. He stayed in his apartment and didn't talk to hardly anyone. Well, anyone except Terrell. Terrell called him every day to see how he was doing and to try and get him out and about and was telling him constantly that it was a team loss and not just his fault. To me that says he is a good teammate and a true friend to Tony Romo!! Did you hear about all of this in the mainstream media? Nope!! Did ESPN report how Terrell Owens the man (not Terrell Owens the football player) was trying to help his friend feel better? A resounding NO!! I was able to find this only because I am a person that pays very close attention to the Cowboys and I am a subscriber to many of the Dallas Cowboys websites and I am able to read what Dallas's local media says about the team.

Fast-forward to present day. The Cowboys missed the playoffs for the 2008-2009 NFL season. And the media is blaming Terrell Owens for the lack of his leadership, the lack of his locker room presence, and his negative attitude. This guy is a true professional that wants the ball. He wants the ball because when he gets it good things happen for him and the team. The media says that is selfish. The media wants us all to believe that he is just looking to get his numbers up because he just wants to be the center of attention and he wants to look good. Damn the team and damn his teammates. That is not true. First off to be a professional wide receiver in the NFL you have to be somewhat narcissistic. If I owned a team I wouldn't want a wide receiver on my team if he didn't want the ball all the time. That shows a lack of confidence in your own skill. I want my guys competing to get open and get the ball because that shows heart and Terrell Owens has heart. Our media is just jumping on the trash Terrell Owens bandwagon because that is what sells right now.

The media wants Terrell Owens cut and out of football. Yeah right!! Who would they report on then? If Terrell

Owens was not on the Cowboys and out of the NFL it would be a slow time in the media shortly thereafter. But because Terrell Owens is such a hot subject they are making up stories saying he will be released or traded. A lot of people here where I work ask me constantly if I care if Terrell is going to be cut. They also make fun of me because a few years ago Terrell Owens is the guy that desecrated the star on the 50 yard line in a game when he was with the San Francisco 49'ers. They also are the same people telling me that he blew up the Philadelphia Eagles locker room with his antics. Are these items true? Yes with a "but". Yes he desecrated the star during that game. But he was showing his San Francisco teammates that even in Dallas he can be a force and he is there to win and was not intimidated. Yes, the Eagles locker room self destructed and blew up and he was a part of it. But, he also broke his leg in the season finale against the Cowboys and was back in time for the Superbowl, way ahead of when doctors said he would and he even signed a paper releasing the Eagles of any future money just so he could play in the Superbowl. Which he did play in with stitches still in his leg from the surgery to put in pins to stabilize it, and later in the game bleeding through his stitches and subsequently his sock. He also led the team in receptions and yards in that game. That to me says more about what kind of man he is as opposed to the man the media portrays him as.

With the NFL draft coming up the media is constantly reporting how Terrell Owens is going to be cut or traded from the Cowboys. They are also reporting that if cut no other team will want to sign him because of his attitude. As I have proven it is not his attitude that is the problem.

It is his persona that the media helped create. They build people up and put them on a pedestal only so they can knock them off of it.

The media got their wish on February 5ᵗʰ 2009. Terrell Owens was cut by the Dallas Cowboys. The media keeps talking about sources telling them that Terrell was a negative influence on the team and that he was distracting too much from the team. The funny thing is that every single time an actual interview showed up from Jerry Jones (owner of the Cowboys) all he had to say about Terrell was positive things. To show how much Terrell meant to him Jerry Jones flew down to Florida to talk to Terrell in person and explain everything to him face to face. That tells me that Terrell wasn't cut from the team for the reasons the media stated. We may never know the whole truth as to why this happened but I believe that it was because of the media and the influence it had on Jerry Jones.

I know I was just talking about Terrell Owens mostly and I threw in Tony Romo in there to show how the media makes Terrell look bad, but I am now going to talk about Tony Romo himself for a second. This guy started dating one of the hottest women in our country Jessica Simpson. (Can't blame the guy there at all can you? I know I can't!!) Suddenly she shows up at a Thanksgiving Day game and they lose. Everybody in the media blames her for him playing bad. She was the reason he threw interceptions. She was distracting to him and the team. At least that is what the media would like you to believe. They publicized the heck out of the fact that he played bad because of her. I couldn't turn on ESPN without reports pointing out that she was there and he played bad because of her being there. The next game the Cowboys were away and the fans at this stadium are wearing Jessica Simpson masks to try and "fluster" Tony into playing poorly. How many players in the NFL play poorly when their wives, girlfriends, or parents are there?

Fast forward 2 years and our media is still talking about how Jessica is a distraction and she is the reason that Tony isn't winning and that he is more focused on her than the team. Again I know the Cowboys, I know about Tony Romo, that guy is a competitor and he wants to win more than anyone but he is entitled to a life outside of football and apparently the media doesn't agree. They want his life put on every page because it sells. He is the quarterback of America's team. His greatness, misfortunes, and love life are big sellers and after all is said and done that is what the media is looking to do? Sell, sell, sell!

Another example of an athlete in the public eye that has his personal life thrown all over the media is Michael Phelps. Here is a man that bleeds red white and blue. The man has 16 medals from the 2004 and 2008 Olympics, which includes 14 gold and 2 bronze metals. With 8 gold metals from the 2008 Olympics. He holds 7 world records in swimming, he was on Wheaties boxes, he was on Saturday Night Live, and countless talk shows. He is truly the all American boy. Then he showed his weak human side. A few months after the Olympics he visited the University of South Carolina and took a hit of marijuana from a bong at party there. To top it off someone took a picture of it. Boom!! The media is all over it. Should he have his medals taken away they scream? Should he be arrested in South Carolina for smoking illegal drugs they asked?

Do I think what Michael did was wrong? Yes I do. (I can honestly say I have never tried any illegal drugs in my life and I never will). But should we destroy a man's whole life because he made one mistake. I mean come on, this guy is only 23 years old. What do you expect from a 23 year old kid? Why was he hanging out at a college party with people his own age? (Hope you got the sarcasm in that last one.) Did our media actually think he was going to sit there and play checkers the rest of his life? We are all human. We all make mistakes but we are all not in the public eye like Michael Phelps is. This kid seems genuine when he says he is sorry for what he did and he is willing to take his 3 month no swimming punishment and loss of Kellogg's endorsement like a man. I say let him take his punishments and leave the guy alone already. Let those without sin cast the first stone.

What I am basically saying here is that our media lacks creativity, honesty, compassion, and just plain and simple smarts!! Of all the people in this world these so called journalists are the best we have? I am going to say this in big bold letters...**SHUT THE HELL UP ALREADY MEDIA!! QUIT REPORTING ONLY THE BAD THINGS. A POSITIVE ATTITUDE WILL GO A VERY LONG WAY TO ECONOMIC RECOVERY!! START POINTING TO THE POSITIVES THAT ARE HAPPENING IN OUR ECONOMY AND STOP BEATING THE NEGATIVITY DEAD HORSE ALREADY!** I learned at a young age if you do not have anything positive to say don't say anything at all. I know that is not possible to stop reporting bad news but throw more good in than bad.

Here is yet another disclaimer for you: I am sure you have noticed I have quoted the media a lot in this book. And you may think that makes me a hypocrite. In a way it does. But what choice do I have? I have to use the means that are available to me. I have to go by what is said in the media. However, I truly research both sides of the story and form my opinion based on everything I look at and not just one or even two things. I form an educated decision based on all the information I gather. I just hope this book opens your eyes like my eyes have been opened doing the research for this book.

Speaking of eye opening experiences the next chapter will hopefully open your eyes to another thing in this country that is MESSED UP...

DISCRIMINATION AND RACISM

This chapter deserves an extra warning...what you are about to read contains some racial comments and it will seem as if this chapter at first is a very negative chapter...please read the whole chapter before coming to any conclusions. OK, now that the warning is over I will get to the meat of the chapter.

There are a lot of things that upset me right now in this world. (If you made it this far you know what I am saying is true.) Discrimination is one of them. Do I believe there is discrimination today? Hell yes!! However it isn't just 1 or 2 races being discriminated against, it is all races. Whether you are black, white, Hispanic, Asian, European, or East Indian, you have experienced discrimination in one way shape or form. Now I know a lot of the non Caucasian people are out there saying that is not true. They are probably saying it is only blacks, or it is only Hispanics, and so on. Once again I will prove my point to you. Hate me if you must but I am not going to lie or sugar coat anything. Discrimination is plain and simple and I don't care who or what you are.

You will always be a human being in my eyes but racism and discrimination has to stop for all.

Martin Luther King Jr. on August 28, 1963 gave his famous "I have a dream" speech. To this day I think this is probably one of the most famous and noteworthy speeches of all time. There is one excerpt that I would like to put here... "I have a dream that one day this nation will rise up and live out the true meaning of it's creed: 'We hold these truths to be self-evident that all men are created equal.'" Equal is the key word in that speech.

All men and women in this country and world are equal in my eyes and always will be until proven otherwise. (We all know some people that are nothing but jerks and assholes. Those people are not equal in my eyes they are lower than me.) Equal, what does that mean? In this instance it means to me the same as me and everyone else. Not better than and not worse than the other. I don't deserve better treatment from anyone in this world because I am a white man. I also don't deserve to be treated any less than anyone because I am a white man. Nobody deserves to be treated any better than anyone else...PERIOD!!

When Martin Luther King Jr. made that speech he wanted a hand of brotherly love extended to all people in this country no matter the race, color, creed, or nationality. He didn't want a hand out as a charity case. He wanted equality. This is where I have a problem. There are people in this world that don't want equality. They want special treatment because of what color, creed, or nationality they are. They want to get into schools because of their situation and not based on their merit. They want the job because of what color, creed, or nationality they are and not because they are the best man or woman for the job. I am going to give you a very interesting point of view on this.

A few years ago Rev. Jesse Jackson went to the commissioner of the NFL and said he wants more black coaches in the NFL and that the NFL is discriminating against black coaches because there are not enough of them. (According to the 2006 census 12.1% of all Americans are blacks. Just a stat I thought I would throw in here.) Because of this the NFL instituted the "Rooney Rule". This rule states that no head coach can be hired by any team without that team seriously interviewing a black coach first. Is this racism? I think so. According to title VII set forth in the civil rights act of 1964, employers are not to discriminate when hiring based on race. That means that the NFL could have been punished by violating that constitutional amendment. However, they were not punished by the government because the NFL did nothing wrong. They truly hired the best man for the job regardless of race.

I would actually like to propose a solution to Mr. Jackson that will make everyone happy. The NFL must have one third of all the coaches in the league be black. In return one third of all players must be white. I'll let that sink in for a moment. Yep you read it right. One third of all coaches black and one third of all players white. I think that is fair don't you? I am willing to bet Mr. Jackson doesn't think it would be fair at all. He would probably say that players that play in the NFL are the best at their jobs regardless of their color and that it would be unfair to cut a black player so a white player could play and meet the quota. To that I say you are right Mr. Jackson. It is not right to make you hire a coach based on color and it is not right have a player on your team based on just color. The best man for the job at hand is what is necessary, not the best black man or the best white man. The best man period!! Jesse Jackson only cares about what is best for him. He is a big hypocrite. Here is proof of Mr. Jackson's hypocrisy. In July 2008 the Rev. Jesse Jackson (is he really a reverend? If so what church is he a reverend for? Just curious about that.) said he wanted to "cut his (Barack Obama's) nuts off for talking down to black people". He later apologized for what he said. What he really apologized for is the fact he got caught saying it on television. He wasn't apologizing for what he said at all. He may have said he was, but he was lying through his teeth. Oh, and get this! When Barack Obama won the election he was shown in the crowd crying his eyes out. Do you think he was crying because Barack Obama was the best man and he voted for him for being the best candidate. Or do you think he was crying because he wanted the publicity for being there to witness the first black president in U.S. History? (Just to let you know I did vote for Barack Obama for president. Not because he was black like Jesse did, but because I believed he was the best man for the job!!)

I remember reading an article a few years ago (unfortunately I can't find it on line right now.) that had a black student suing a university because they didn't have enough black students. So he wanted to be admitted over a more qualified student. This particular student had poor test scores. He had a poor high school transcript. This delusional young man actually believed he belonged in this school over a more qualified student because of his skin color. Is this truly what Dr. King wanted? No!!! He wanted equality. Not special treatment. Dr. King wanted everyone to be truly equal. He did not want a hand out he wanted an extended hand in brotherly love. We will never get past discrimination as long as we keep looking for the free lunch. Stop looking for a reason as to why you didn't get into the school, didn't get the job, or you didn't get the loan you applied for. Just once I want to see a person on Maury Povich or Oprah stand up and say "I wasn't discriminated against because of my skin color, my sex, or my sexual preference for that matter. I am just a shit head! And I didn't deserve that job because I wasn't qualified."

How do we get away from discrimination you might be asking? That is a long, winding road that will require a lot of people doing the right thing.

I think one thing that needs to be done is to stop using discriminatory terms to refer to your own people. I can't tell you how many movies, comedy shows, TV shows, and just ordinary people on the street use terms that are racist and towards themselves. How can we as a nation stop using these words when you are using them yourselves to describe your own people? I am flabbergasted at one particular TV show that just came out on comedy central. The show is "Chocolate News" starring David Allen Greer. I watched this show once (just once)and was just shaken to see a black man make fun of his race. He did this by using stereotypes, vulgar language, and just plain stupidity. Why would anyone want to do this? Again I ask is this what Dr. King wanted?

Even Bill Cosby himself spoke up about racist comments. "Racism continues to exist" he said "but, there is nothing that will defeat good parenting!" Later on in his speech he said "They are standing on a street corner and they can't speak English" he then said "I can't even talk the way these people talk: 'Why you ain't,' 'Where you is'...and I blamed the kid, until I heard the mother talk. And then I heard the father talk." Cosby was criticized for his comments. He was told he was pointing out that blacks are to blame for losing the battles. To which he responded "Come at me all you want, I know a victim when I see one. And so did Christ. And so does God know victims. And so do we all recognize victims. But some victims you can look at and say 'Get up'".

Truer words could not have been spoken. This message goes out to all in the United States. Not just the "minorities". Stop the victim mentality. Yes, some of our ancestors were brought here under the wrong terms. They braved slavery. They braved severe racism and discrimination early in our country's life. We as a country are better because of what they were able to live through. Do not soil the soul of our ancestors by insisting that you are owed something for the suffering that they did. You are here in the best country in the world and that was made possible by their sacrifices.

Discrimination goes against all races as I stated above. For example a man (a white man) in Buffalo NY was awarded 150,000 dollars in a racial discrimination lawsuit in 2007. He worked for the state and was dismissed from his job because he couldn't tolerate being called names like "cracker," "pollock" "and stupid white boy." According to the court records this guy's supervisor was fined 2000 dollars after they investigated these allegations in 1998. The white employee was later dismissed in 1999. (It took the court system 8 years to get this guy money, what a crock!!)

I work with Polish legal immigrants here. These people have told me stories of how they have been discriminated against because of their polish accent. And how they have had to endure people calling them names where they worked, where they shopped, and even where they lived. Is this really what this country has come to? Unless your name is something like Sitting Bull, or another native American name, you also come from another country besides here.

Discrimination isn't just about race anymore. It is actually about putting people down and trying to keep them down by using anything and everything against them. It isn't just color anymore. It could be their nationality, it could be their voice, their hair, how they walk, how they talk, and God knows what else.

I once experienced discrimination at its finest. I worked for a dealership where the owner was a black woman. This part didn't bother me. What bothered me is how she obtained that dealership. (I am going to give an example here that isn't exact figures but it does follow the general idea.) For arguments sake lets say to buy this particular brand of car dealership you had to have a bachelors degree in business, invest 10 million dollars, have 10 years experience in the automobile business, and go through the ownership training program. She did 2 out of the 4. She had the degree and she went through the ownership training program, but didn't have the money and had no prior dealership experience. She was rushed through the program to get her a dealership as soon as possible because she was black and a woman. After 5 years of owning this dealership she practically ran it into the ground.

She wound up selling it to a more experienced car dealer. Do you think it was fair that she got this opportunity because of what she was and not who she was? I certainly don't. I worked for this woman for 6 months and during this 6 months she did not run this dealership like it needed to be run. She ran it like she thought she should but because she had no prior dealership experience. It just didn't work. I got out of there after 6 months based on this fact. I feared for my income and I feared for my families well being. The sad part is I was right. A lot of people lost their jobs because they relied on their boss to do the right thing for the company but she didn't. They lost their jobs because this auto maker decided it was more important to put a black woman in charge. They should have been concerned with putting the right person in this position. I am sure that there were a lot more qualified persons looking for a dealership than this woman. But she got the leg up because of what she was and not for who she was. Do you really think this is what Dr. King wanted?

There is one other type of discrimination that is running still in this country. That is sexual discrimination. Sexual discrimination is not just for women anymore. Granted most cases of sexual discrimination are men discriminating against women but it has happened where women discriminate against men also. The difference is most men won't come forward because of fear of being persecuted or made fun of. Most men think of a man having a woman in power telling them what to do is a dream but it can be a nightmare to for a happily married man.

I seem to remember a great movie named **DISCLOSURE.** This movie starred Michael Douglas and Demi Moore. In this movie Demi Moore was put in charge of the company Michael Douglas worked for. One night she invited him to stay late so they could work on a project together. But, because they had a relationship in the past she was interested in him in more ways than just business. (Lucky bastard) While he was making a call she made sexual advances toward him that he kept refusing (yeah you know this is fiction). Over and over again he said no to her, but she kept going at him. He never hung up the phone so the person he called had it all on tape (the person he was calling wasn't home so it made it to his answering machine.) Once he refused her advances things were different around the office. She would exclude him from meetings. And when he filed a suit against the company she filed a counter suit saying he harassed her. In the end this tape of him saying no surfaced and he won. The one thing that stuck out in my mind during the proceedings was the statement (paraphrased) sexual harassment is about power. When did he have the power? The fact is you set the meeting time, you set the meeting place, and you ordered the wine. He never had the power you were the boss, you wanted him, and you were upset when you couldn't have him. (Again that is not the exact phrase but you can see what I mean).

I am not saying that men have it worse than women. I was just giving an example of how it could go either way. I know women do have to deal with discrimination a lot more than men. I truly do believe this to be true. I know because I see it everywhere I go. I have seen it in my own business. I worked at a dealership where if a woman walked in without a man with her salespeople wouldn't even approach her to say hello. If they actually did wind up talking to a salesperson these guys would actually ask her to call her husband for approval or just plain ask her if she needed his permission to go forward with the decision. I also watched these same salespeople when a man and woman came in together they would talk strictly to the man. It didn't matter that studies show that the woman has more to do with the actual car buying than the men do.

I remember one car commercial where a young lady was looking for her first car and the salesperson pointed out the visor mirror so she could check her makeup and when she asked what kind of safety features the car had he said "this car is very safe" insinuating that she wouldn't understand anything he was going to tell her about the safety features of the car.

I have also seen the opposite happen. I have worked with many salespeople in my long 18 year career in the automobile sales business. Some of these salespeople have indeed been sales women and I have seen them discriminate toward the men. I have seen one particular saleswoman I worked with say to a male customer "are you sure your wife will like this color?", and other questions along those lines. I will also tell you this...I have seen women customers treat our women salespeople like crap because they think there is no way a woman could be knowledgeable about the car. I have even seen women get upset at their husband because he was talking to the woman salesperson, like she was threatened by another woman attempting to sell her husband a car. I have said this a few times here....DISCRIMINATION IS DISCRIMINATION and it doesn't matter who it is coming from or who it is being directed toward it should not be tolerated.

I am sitting here talking to a friend of mine right now about discrimination and racism. He said I have to bring up the fact that O.J. Simpson literally got away with murder. The reason he got away with it was because he was a rich black man that lived in L.A. This is a case of our media (I know it is not the media chapter but I still think it fits here.) influencing a verdict. It was reported that if O.J. was convicted it would be all about race and the black community would riot and cause more problems than just one black murder being set free. It would be another example of the white justice system shutting down the black man yet again. If he is not convicted it was reported that white people would say it is because of what happened to Rodney King in L.A. and that the judicial system is scared of offending the black community. This is exactly what happened. This alone is a case of racism and discrimination. Apparently our government is scared more of what the black community thinks as opposed to what the white community thinks. It is not reverse racism. Racism is racism it doesn't matter the color of a person.

That is what I am talking about here. Man or woman, black or white, born in America or immigrated here, it doesn't matter; we all should be treated equally. We are all here for life, liberty, and the pursuit of happiness. We all should be allowed to do it without this discrimination.

People have come to this country to get away from all of this discrimination. People in this country should be tolerant of all people no matter who they are, what they are(unless they are assholes like I said earlier, asshole isn't a race, sex, or nationality, it is a choice),what color they are, or where they come from. We are all a part of this wonderful country. Lets all make it better for everyone here. And again that means we are ALL EQUAL!!

Speaking of people coming to America. That brings us to...

IMMIGRATION

This country was founded by immigrants and immigrants are the backbone of our society. However, all immigrants should be subject to the same rules as everyone else. You need to become a citizen. You need to pay your taxes. You need to learn English.

I am going to start there. I am so sick of calling places and having this come on the phone "for English press 1.... for Spanish press 2" (para espanol pulse dos [thank you Google translator]). How bout we do this instead. "for English press 1...for any other language go to school and learn English. Or go back to the country that speaks what you speak!!" I know you are going to say that I was just preaching about how discrimination needs to go away and that I am now discriminating against people that do not speak English. Why should they not be entitled to speak whatever language they want in this country you may be asking? Let me explain. I promise you that if you go to another country they will not give you the option of what language to speak. If you go to Mexico you better be able to speak some Spanish. (Unless you are in a tourist resort. Then they speak the international language of the all mighty dollar.) If you go to France be prepared to speak French or they will have you for lunch over their. I have been to a few countries in the course of my life. Let me tell you something if you don't speak the language of that country it is very difficult to get around and talk to people, find what you are looking for, or even eat.

That reminds me of a very funny story that happened to me in Cancun Mexico. While on the resort grounds it was easy because everyone spoke English. However my girlfriend and I decided to go to the market place where we could get stuff by negotiating the price. I am good at bargaining and negotiating given my career and all. I want you to keep in mind that my girlfriend (who wound up being my wife later on...I actually proposed to her in Cancun on this trip. But more on her in the next chapter.) was a Mexican-American. Her whole family spoke Spanish (Americanized Spanish anyway)fluently. So anyway, we took the bus to the market place and spent about 2 hours there. We got some really good deals after hammering these guys. It was like they never knew what hit them! But that is not the funny part. The funny part happened when we left. We walked out and couldn't find the bus stop. We walked for almost 5 hours in downtown Cancun. And if you ever walked in downtown Cancun and looked around you would be as concerned/scared as I was. It was now starting to get dark out. I kept asking people where I could find the number 3 bus back to the resort area. (I preferred buses because I heard the stories of Americans being driven out to nowhere in cabs and robbed. Also the buses were a lot cheaper.) Nobody understood what I was asking for. They kept trying to speak to me in Spanish and my girlfriend didn't catch all they said before the people walked away. Then I saw the answer. A Cancun police officer. There he was standing on a corner waiting to cross the street. I asked my girlfriend to go ask him in Spanish where the bus stop was. Her exact answer was "I can't do that" to which I replied "why not?" she said "I won't understand him." that stunned me. So I asked "what the hell did I bring you along for then". She said the Spanish she knows is not the same as what they spoke and they speak too fast for her to understand the little bit she could make out. Needless to say we wound up taking the next cab back to the resort and never went back in downtown Cancun again.

The other countries that I visited could give two shits about us as a whole. I personally have never been to France but the people I know that have been there have told me how they look down on Americans. (I think I shall take this chance to point out if not for our American soldiers you would be speaking German not French, so wake up and show some respect!!) France sure doesn't look down on us when they need something that is for sure.

We as a country, have more people coming in here than any other country like I previously stated. And it is because of this we have an immigration problem. We have too many people here in America that are not here legally. I am not just referring to people from Mexico. I knew a woman from the Philippines that was here for over 10 years and was living and working with a "temporary" social security number she received when she first got here. She never ever went to get her permanent status changed or apply to be a citizen. This woman was able to work as a computer graphics designer and own a home in the United States but was not a legal citizen or even a legal immigrant with a "green card". How is that possible you may ask? I wish I knew!! All I know is that it is possible. And if I know one person like this there must be thousands or even millions throughout the whole country living on a social security number that is just temporary.

As I already told you I am a finance manager for a car dealer full time. Because of this position I have seen many things. I have had on numerous occasions come across people using someone else's name and social security number to try and buy a car. But I must tell you about one specific time that just happened to me within the last year. We had a Hispanic gentleman here attempting to purchase a new car from us. We checked his previous credit history and it looked pretty good. (We were able to do this because he filled out an application for credit.) He had approximately 4000 dollars to use as a down payment. I proceeded to submit the application for approval with our lender. I got an approval with a couple stipulations. Those stipulations were that this gentleman needed to provide me with a copy of his social security card and proof of his job with a pay stub. Pretty reasonable requests for a legitimate car purchase. Especially one that is requiring finance. Well low and behold he brought in both and both the pay stub and social security card had different numbers on them. Now here is the funny part of this story. His name was the same on both papers and none of these numbers were the number he provided on his application. I brought this man into my office because this was one story I had to hear. I proceeded to ask him how this was possible. Now get this....he said the number he gave me on the application was his but it was temporary number that had expired. The card he had was one that a friend of his made for him when he got to this country and the number on the pay stub was his cousin's who is a legal resident. So this man was working on his cousin's social security number, showing authorities a fake one, and living in the United States on an expired temporary social security. Needless to say I alerted immigration. Why should this man be allowed to live here illegally? Not to mention work here illegally.

That is where I have the biggest problem. The fact that we have illegal immigrants working here most of the time for cash without taxes being taken out of that income. This particular guy that I just spoke of was having taxes taken out but I am sure he wasn't physically filing his taxes every April 15th like the rest of us.

A few Americans will say again that this isn't right. Well to them I say keep reading.

Here are some facts for you to think about. One of our biggest problems in this country is medical expenses. Let's ask the Mexican government to do for us what we do for the Mexican immigrants. Do you think they will? I don't think so. An illegal immigrant is allowed to do everything we are allowed to do except vote. An illegal immigrant is allowed the same medical benefits we tax paying citizens are.

I am going to include an article here from CNN. com. This article was published April 10, 2006.

"(CNN) -- Hundreds of thousands of protesters turned out Monday in small towns and big cities across

the United States, demanding that undocumented immigrants get a chance to live the American dream.

Organizers said their "national day of action for immigration justice" included events in more than 140 cities in at least 39 states, with drum-banging and flag-waving masses chanting "Si se puede" -- "Yes we can" -- in rallies from coast to coast.

The events served as a visible demonstration of political clout for supporters of the nation's estimated 11-12 million undocumented immigrants.

"The sleeping giant is awake -- wide awake -- and we're paying close attention," said Jaime Contreras, president of the National Capital Immigration Coalition, one of the groups involved in organizing the demonstrations.

The protests began in the morning in communities on the East Coast, then spread across the country throughout the day and continued into the evening.

Two of the largest demonstrations were held in Washington, D.C., and Phoenix, Arizona. Organizers said 500,000 attended the event in Washington and 200,000 in Phoenix, although police did not provide official crowd estimates.

In a nod to criticism of demonstrators who waved foreign flags at earlier pro-immigration rallies, the Stars and Stripes were on prominent display at many of Monday's events.

In Washington, protesters held up signs proclaiming, "We Are America."

"What we want to achieve is to send a very strong message to the Senate, to the Congress in general and this

administration that immigrants are fed up, that we are tired, that we work very hard," Contreras said.

"We come to this country not to take from America, but to make America strong. And we do not deserve to be treated the way we have been treated," he said. 'We are not criminals'

The nationwide protests drew a cool response from one of the House's leading proponents of reducing immigration.

Rep. Tom Tancredo, a Colorado Republican, said the demonstrations show "how entrenched the illegal alien lobby has become."

Some counter-protests were also held Monday by people who favor stricter immigration laws, but they paled in size and scope next to the pro-immigration rallies.

In Atlanta, a crowd estimated by police at 30,000 to 40,000 gathered outside a suburban shopping mall that serves the area's growing Latino population. Organizers had asked demonstrators to wear white T-shirts, and the gathering looked like a sea of white from the air.

Alluding to the city's history as the cradle of the civil rights movement, demonstrators carried a sign reading "We Have A Dream, Too."

In Los Angeles, California, Cardinal Roger Mahony, the city's Roman Catholic archbishop, urged lawmakers to pass immigration reform that includes a path to legalization for "all undocumented residents."

"We are all God's children, united for a just immigration reform," Mahony said. "We all deserve respect and care."

In New York, thousands of people rallied outside City Hall, waving flags from countries as close as Mexico and as far away as Bangladesh.

Undocumented Mexican immigrant Ana Sanchez and her children wore shirts that read: "We are not criminals."

"I'm coming for work. I want to work," said protester John Cervantes, an illegal immigrant from Ecuador whose daughter, Evelyn, is a citizen born in the United States.

Grassroots forces

Monday's protests are part of a wave of demonstrations in recent weeks, as Congress grapples with the thorny issue of how to overhaul the nation's immigration system.

Credit for driving the protests has been given to grassroots forces such as union and church leaders, Spanish-language radio hosts and students sending text messages to spread plans for school walkouts.

Harry Pachon, an expert on Latino politics at the University of Southern California, said the growing wave of demonstrations shows that a "pan-Latino identity is beginning to show itself."

"It caught many Hispanic leaders by surprise, because this is really a working community's demonstrations," he said.

"The immigration debate up to these demonstrations has largely been one-sided. It's been very hard for anyone to argue for the undocumented immigrant."

Bush: Strong feelings

In Washington, President Bush said Monday's rallies were "a sign that this is an important issue that people feel strongly about."

The president has been pushing Congress to pass legislation that includes a temporary guest-worker provision for non citizens.

"People ought to be here on a ... temporary basis. And if they want to become a citizen, after a series of steps they've got to take, they get in line, like everybody else; not at the head of the line, but the end of the line," he said.

The immigration issue has put Bush and many lawmakers in a difficult position, with uncertain political consequences.

Bush has made reaching out to Latinos a priority, making inroads in what has traditionally been a Democratic constituency.

But he and other Republican leaders must also contend with a growing chorus within their conservative base to crack down on illegal immigration.

Senate legislation last week was hailed as a breakthrough in the immigration debate, but the compromise drafted by Republican Sens. Chuck Hagel of Nebraska and Mel Martinez of Florida failed to gain enough support in a vote before a two-week recess.

But on Monday, Sen. Hillary Clinton told a rally in New York she was "convinced that we will have immigration reform because it makes sense for America."

"But not the kind of legislation that was passed in the House, because that is not in keeping with either reality or American values," the New York Democrat said.

The House in December passed immigration legislation that has drawn fierce opposition from Latino groups. It calls for building a 700-mile-long security fence on the U.S.-Mexico border and for making illegal immigration a felony.

The House bill contains neither of the provisions in the Senate legislation that have divided Republicans -- the guest-worker program and a process allowing illegal immigrants to pursue legal status to stay in the country and obtain citizenship.

If the Senate manages to pass a bill after its recess, a joint committee of members of the House and Senate would have to reach a compromise.

Tancredo is among the critics who consider the Senate's proposed legalization process to be "amnesty." Supporters call it "earned citizenship."

*"Amnesty is an affront to American law and America's tradition of legal immigration," Tancredo said in a written statement. "If the protesters really want to honor America's values, they would stand up to law*breakers *and embrace an enforcement-first approach to fixing our broken system."*

Now that you have read the same article I am sure you can see why I posted the whole article. But just in case you don't see my point of this article I have posted my response to it below.

After reading this article I felt like I just had to put it in my book. The thing that stood out in my mind were the fact that the people didn't think they were breaking the law by working and living here illegally. And, the other comment that stuck out in my mind was the one saying that the 11 – 12 million estimated illegal immigrants in this country have political clout. How is that possible? How can somebody without the right to vote have any political clout? How can these people be talking out about our immigration policies?

I can not believe I am about to side with politicians here but I agree that illegal immigration should be a felony. People should be punished for not following the laws of the United States of America. You want to live in America you must abide by the laws of the country. You need to become a citizen in this country. You need to follow the laws to make you a citizen. I just can not believe how lenient we are on this situation. Why are we allowing people to live and work here illegally?

There was one man that said " I came to this country for work and I want to work." That is great. We want you to work too. But we want you to get citizenship here and work here and pay taxes here. Another man said that they want to send a message that immigrants work hard and are fed up with the way they are treated. He also said "We come to this country not to take from America, but to make America strong. And we do not deserve to be treated the way we have been treated." If you truly don't like how you are being treated, leave. Go back where you came from. Do not pass go do not collect 200 dollars.

Let me get this straight. You don't want to take from America. That must mean you want to give to America. So you are paying your federal taxes to the American government. You are giving your social security taxes to the government so the people in this country that need it can get it. Oh, you must be giving your special skill that you, and only you, possess that makes you valuable to this country and irreplaceable. I am sure the answer to those questions are no, no, and no. Based on those answers let me tell you what you are taking. You are taking money for working here and not paying any taxes on them. You are taking a job from a legal immigrant or an American citizen. You are taking free medical care. I know I can be really harsh at times but I am pointing out the obvious to people. How does not being a legal citizen make America strong? I would love to hear that argument.

The other part of this article that was shocking to me is that police officers were there and they knew some of these people protesting were illegal and they didn't bring them in. I know, I know, there were thousands upon thousands of people there how could they get all of them? That is the beauty of it you didn't have to get all of them. You just had to get some of them to show that you mean business.

I can not believe that I am about to side with George W. Bush on his statement " People ought to be here on a ... temporary basis. And if they want to become a citizen, after a series of steps they've got to take, they get in line, like everybody else; not at the head of the line, but the end of the line." I must point out again I am for immigration and feel it truly is the backbone of this country and immigration is part of what makes this country great. But everybody should have to follow the rules and regulations that are made to help all that come here, and all that are already here.

I can not believe that one of our own congressman actually thinks that the illegal immigrant lobby is entrenched. Entrenched? Really? Who cares? They can't even vote. I am about to mix two of my chapters here. I had a personal debate with myself about where to put what I am about to show you. It involves the economy and immigration. I will let you decide if I put it in the right place. (The two chapters in question are immigration and economy)

Everybody wants to be politically correct and say that it is OK that this is happening. Well I am not always politically correct. I am not OK with this happening. I am far from OK with this happening. We need a law that is going to stop this or at least slow it down and keep this money here.

Like I said, I am all for immigration. I love the diversity our country has because of immigration. I want everyone in the world to have the opportunity to live the lives they want to live, but I want it done the correct and legal way.

In yet another article dated February 10, 2009 on CNN.com, a man named Pedro Pablo from Guatemala said he is going back to Guatemala because he can not make it here as an illegal immigrant. He worked only 3 days over the last year and can not afford to send any money to his wife and 5 sons in Guatemala. He even told CNN that he thought he could get ahead here and that he now regrets coming to America.

Here is a man that worked here for 4 years and didn't pay taxes and almost all the money he made was sent to another country and was spent there and not here. He lived in a 1 bedroom apartment with 7 other men. (7 men in a one bedroom apartment, pardon my language but holy shit!! My 15 year old daughter has a problem with her 8 year old sister wanting to sleep in her room with her.) Pedro said his bed was a corner in the living room where he kept his duffel bag and blanket. Well Pedro had you done things right you might have had a better paying job with benefits and not had to worry about only working 3 days. And who knows you might have actually been able to bring your wife and 5 sons over here with the money you made as a legal citizen. I say good bye to you Pedro and wish you the best, but I am glad you are no longer taking money from us here.

In this same article it is stated that in 2007 26 billion dollars was sent to Mexico from people that were here legally and illegally. That number fell to 25 billion in the year 2008. This money came from people that have immigrated here legally and illegally. And think about this; that is only the money that was sent to Mexico. What about the money sent to Poland? Columbia? India? Or even China? How much more money is sent to those countries? A professor at Florida International University named Erik Camayd-Freixas took a recent trip to Guatemala where he saw the effect of less money being sent there by immigrants. "Everybody was talking about it." He said "The local Economies are severely impacted by it and unemployment is running rampant." Well Mr. Camayd-Freixas. I do not care about what is happening in Guatemala. I care about what is happening here. I care that Pedro worked here for 4 years and not only did he not pay taxes on the money he made here, he also sent money to his "home country". And our country is losing jobs because our money is not being spent at an American retailer and in turn that retailer is not paying taxes on that money.

We need a law to prevent money from being earned here and sent overseas. This situation is causing this country to lose millions and millions of dollars, hell even billions, in consumer spending every year. And this is causing job losses. It is common sense people!! Less money spent here means less products being bought. Less products being bought means less products that need to be produced. Less products being produced means less people needed to make those products. Less people needed to make those products means less jobs needed, and that means less taxes coming in and it means less money staying here. Once again I think this makes way too much sense for anyone in government to understand it and do something about it. Money makes our world go round.

I am actually starting to believe that illegal immigrants actually have more rights than American citizens. Well, maybe not more rights but they get treated with the same rights we have. I don't believe this is right at all. Yes, I have another example for you.

I will be   paraphrasing article written October 19, 2001 written by J. Zane Walley for Worldnetdaily to explain my point.

On September 23, 2001 a man named John Petrello was notified by his friend and neighbor Phil Mathews that fourteen illegal aliens had been dropped off from a truck practically in his back yard. He immediately told his wife Dorothy to call the border patrol. While she was doing just that he and Phil went outside to confront the aliens with guns in hand.

See John had run into a problem at an earlier date where he had been forced to fire shots at twelve backpacked Mexican illegals who were then running at his pregnant wife and 3 year old son. He feared the men were drug mules and therefor feared for the safety of his family. He got between the illegals and his family and screamed "alto" (stop in Spanish). They kept coming. He fired 9 shots into the ground in front of them. One man ran back to where he came from the other 11 kept coming. John then fired shots closer to them. "I didn't want to kill anybody" he says "But I needed them to know I was serious. They stopped this time and we looked at one another and I pointed the pistol straight into them. They left at that point.

On this morning when the illegals saw John and Phil coming at them they immediately ran across the road to land belonging to a neighbor. They immediately told the Mexican party to stop, get down on the ground, and lie there. "hablan ingles?" they asked the group. Nobody spoke English or admitted to knowing any English.

As John and Phil kept these men covered, a car riding low on its springs because of all the weight of another group of illegals drove up. John stayed and kept the first group covered while Phil detained the new group. Between the 2 men they held a total of 26 illegals waiting for the border patrol. Once the patrol arrived they asked John and Phil to fill out a report. They then left and took all 26 prisoners with them.

Later that afternoon John and Phil were surprised when they met up with a deputy named Julia Francis. She informed them that the aliens they detained earlier that day were suing John for violating there civil rights. They also lodged a complaint with Miguel Escobar Valdez, the local Mexican consul. John was told he could be subject to arrest in the days to come.

The charges and lawsuit were eventually dropped but that is not the point. The fact that the charges and lawsuit were even considered is appalling. To put an American citizen through the ringer for abiding by the laws of the land and trying to protect his family and land is just plain shitty!!!

So let me get this straight. People that are breaking the law (illegal immigrants) don't get arrested and don't think they are breaking the law. However, people that help the officers uphold the law can get sued by the people that are not citizens and are breaking the law. Tell me that this is not MESSED UP!!

There is a reason you are here in America. You are here to have a better life. You left the country you were in because it is not a good place to be. Whether it is because you couldn't find work, or you feel America is a better place to raise a family, or even if you just got out of being persecuted for your beliefs in the other country. There is a reason you left there, came here, and stayed here!! If you loved your previous country so much why didn't you stay there? If this country is so bad, why don't you go back to the country you came from? It is because even though our system isn't perfect it is still the best in the world. You want what is best for you and your family. I respect that. I truly do. Now please abide by our laws and become legal and do it the right way.

It is good to respect your native country and your heritage. But you can do that without disrespecting your new country. And yes, I do consider it to be your country too. It is not just my country it is everyone's country. We are all here to make this a better place to live.

Is this ever going to end? Seriously? I don't think it will.

I just read another article in the New York times about a woman refugee that has 7 kids. (Yep, I said 7) She said she is having a hard time in America because the government doesn't help her enough. She has a 4 bedroom house in Utah and her rent is $1095. She is making 6 dollars an hour putting price tags on clothes at a second hand clothing store. Do I like the fact that she has 7 (all of which she had before she got here from Somalia.) kids and is having a hard time making ends meet. No, I don't like it, but let's think about this. She came from a country that obviously was worse off than this right? She said "my kids are always asking me for a little bit of money so they can buy a soda after school, and I usually don't have any." Let me ask her this; over in Somalia did your children even go to school? Did they have soda over there? I am willing to bet the answer is no on both counts.

A lot of people here don't get to do extra things that they would like to do because of money. That is how things go. I would also tell her that we all make sacrifices for the betterment of our families. She may be not getting rich but she is giving her children an opportunity she never had. She is sacrificing a lot for her children and that is part of being a parent I believe. And if you are not happy here and your kids are not happy here living off of welfare and any other help you may be receiving, then go back to Somalia!! See what Somalia is willing to give you for your support!! I am willing to bet that it will be nothing at all!!

Did you know that refugees that come here get money from the supplemental security income fund for 7 years. So they get paid for 7 years just to come to America from their crappy country. And now I am reading that because a lot of these people didn't go for naturalization during that 7 years they may lose those benefits. But wait, there's more...they are upset because they are going to lose that money. They have lived here for 7 years, worked here (or not in some cases)for 7 years, gotten money from our government during that 7 years, and all that the government told them is that you have 7 years to become a citizen...and they didn't do that and they are mad about losing the money from the government now. Can you freaking believe that? Sorry to say this, but you don't follow rules, tough shit!! Leave the country and go back to where you came from!! I say SCREW EM!! Do you think your homeland government will give you money for 7 years to come back? I mean come on, we took care of you for 7 years and the one thing we asked you do you didn't do. 7 freakin' years!!! That is a long time. (that is 49 years in dog years) Think about it... your boss says you have 7 years to complete a project at work and says if you don't get it done in that 7 years you have leave his company. How many of us would not do that project? How many of us would want to see if he is bluffing? How much sympathy would your boss have for you if you didn't do that project after the 7 years had expired? I honestly believe that the answer to all those questions is NONE!!!!! Nobody I know would not do that project. Nobody I know would want to see if he is bluffing. And no boss I know would have any sympathy for anyone that didn't do their project in 7 years time.

I would think that the citizenship would be the first thing I would do if I came here compared to the country these people are leaving. These people are refugees. They are not doctors or nurses coming here to make a ton of money and then go back to their respective countries or even stay here after making a ton of money. They are people that are running from persecution, or running for fear of being killed, or coming here to get away from not being able to eat at all. I mean come on people. Wake up!! I have said it before and I will say it again... "You came here for a reason." Now do what is necessary to stay here and make that better life that you wanted.

The funny thing is that all these refugees and illegal immigrants all could be making more money than they are as illegals. They could all be doing better than they currently are by just following the rules. Most illegals in this country get paid cash under the table. Do you really think that these people are making 40 or 50 dollars an hour? No! They are making slave wages because the employer knows they are illegal and they can get away with it.

Do I believe that becoming a citizen is easy? No, I don't think it is. I was born in America. So I am very lucky to say I didn't have to go through the process. However, I do work with people that have been in this country for over 10 years and they are legal citizens here.

They went through the process and they are making a darn good living now. They own homes, cars, and have families. Their kids are going to school and learning and having great childhoods because their parents brought them here and are doing things the right way, the American way, and most importantly the legal way.

It is common sense people. If I am told I will make 50 dollars a day for working 15 hours or I will get paid 6.55 (federal minimum wage) an hour for working 8 hours and then I can get another job for 5 or 6 hours making the same. Where am I better off? And if I do get a minimum wage job that is full time their also will be benefits like health coverage and retirement plans available to me.

Speaking of health coverage....

HEALTH CARE SYSTEM

Who reading this has ever gone to a doctor's office? Now who reading this has ever gone to one doctor's office only to be referred to another doctor's office for tests and then after the tests you have to go back to the original doctor's office to get the results of the test. Then if the tests come back to where you need a surgical procedure you need to go see another doctor to have that done? I know I have had to do this many times. It is sick (pun intended). This particular scenario is just the beginning of our health care systems problems.

Our health care system is so MESSED UP right now it literally does make me want to puke!! There are millions upon millions (an estimated 45 million) in this country without health insurance. The other people who do have health insurance pay through the nose for it and it only covers from 60-80% of what the bill is. Oh and lets not forget the deductible. The health insurance I have now costs me 500 dollars per month (I rounded). It covers me and my kids. There is a 2500 dollar deductible per person and a max of 5000 dollars deductible per family. And after the deductible they pay 80% of the bill. So if I get hurt on the first of the year and the bill is 10,000 dollars I pay the first 2500 dollars. Then they pay 5600 dollars of the remaining 7500 dollars. Which means I will pay another 1900 dollars besides the 2500 for a total of 4400 dollars. Plus my premiums. And then after that for the rest of the year they will pay 80% of all medical bills except "well" care. Well care is physical exams and immunizations. For that they pay 100% and it is not subject to a deductible. So you basically have to be rich to get sick in this country. If you are healthy they will pay for all you need to stay that way.

One example of how our health care system is MESSED UP and not working for all of us is this.

I know a person that was admitted to a hospital to have a minor surgery. During this surgery there were doctors, nurses, and anesthesiologists present. This particular hospital he went to was covered under his insurance plan. There were other hospitals closer to his home but they were not a part of his PPO (preferred provider organization) insurance so he decided it would be best for his wallet to go to the hospital that was covered under the PPO. Anyway he had his surgery and recovered nicely. That is until he got the bill. The doctor and the nurses that were present for the surgery were covered under the PPO. However, my friend received a separate bill from the anesthesiologist and this person was not a part of the hospital and therefor was not covered under his plan at the PPO rate. He was subject to much higher costs for this anesthesiologist. I know this is MESSED UP, right? Here is a man that did everything according to the book but has to pay more because he didn't know that the anesthesiologist wasn't a part of his PPO. What was he supposed to do right before he was given the anesthetic say "hey dude I need to know if you are part of my PPO or not? Can you show me proof that you are?" You have read to this point and you know I think logically. Does this sound like a logical solution? Let's say he did ask that and he found out that indeed he wasn't covered for this particular anesthesiologist? Would he not have the surgery? Would he wait for one that is? Lets be real here people. If you go to a hospital that is listed on your PPO list, all situations involved in your stay at that hospital should be covered under your PPO. There should be no exceptions to this at all!! That is 100% **MESSED UP!!**

A lot of people in our country are screaming that we should adapt to the Canadian way of doing health care. For those of you that don't know about Canada health care I will explain it now.

The Canada Health Act requires that all insured persons be fully insured, without co-payments or user fees, for all medically necessary hospital and physician care. The Canadian government is the main source for funding health care because they play a key role in the insurance market. The government intervention is necessary because they claim that private insurance companies could refuse to insure high risk clients or force them to pay a much higher premium to offset the risk. The Canadian government believes that by them supplying the public with insurance they can avoid unnecessary premium hikes which ultimately effect the health of the people. They also believe that by the government supplying the insurance it will eliminate the economic diversity problem. That means that people with low income get the same coverage as people that make a lot of money. The Canadian government also has eliminated the big overhead that we Americans pay for our insurance, such as the billing and collecting of fees, the marketing of the policies, and the evaluation of insurance risks. I can't tell you the last time I watched television for more than an hour that I didn't see a blue cross blue shield commercial on. Where do you think they get the money for those commercials? That's right, the people that have the insurance pay it out of their premiums, and that makes the premiums higher.

The federal program is done by the federal government issuing money to the individual providences and those providences distribute the money to the various health care providers. The also have the responsibility for health care delivery. This includes for example: determining how many beds will be available in a province; deciding what categories of staff will be hired; determining how the system will serve the population; approving hospital budgets; and negotiating fee scales with the medical association and other health professional organizations.

So let me get this straight, the Canadian government has a right to say how many hospital beds are available to the public? They decide what kind of doctors are available to the hospitals? Not to sound too pessimistic here but do we really want our government deciding these things? I don't know about you but I sure as hell wouldn't want them to have a say in any of my medical situations.

What we need to do is find a happy medium between the current system and the government involved system. And here is that solution. (Come on you knew I would have a solution to this problem, didn't you?)

As I stated earlier I pay 500 dollars per month for my health care provided by my employer. I truly think that I am on the low end here too. What we need is an alternative to our health insurance system. We need a government backed health insurance program. This program will be available to all people in this country, not just the poor and elderly. (i.e. Medicaid and Medicare) The government would not interfere with you selecting your own doctor, your own hospitals, and you can not be turned down for coverage regardless of pre-existing conditions. This insurance would be run by the government. (Yes, I know that sounds scary but keep reading.) The insurance would be a part of our taxes. It would be taken from our taxes. This is the only fair way for all people. The poor, who pay less in taxes, would pay less for insurance than a person that makes more. I know the people that read this will flip out and say "why should I have to pay more than anyone else because I just happen to make more? That isn't fair." Well, let me ask this. Why do you think we pay more for health insurance and overall health care now? It is because you already are paying for people that can not afford health care. You just don't realize it.

How is this you might ask? Well, in this country nobody can be turned away from a hospital's emergency room for lack of ability to pay, and yes that includes illegal immigrants. So people without insurance flock to emergency rooms when all they need is a minor doctor visit. The emergency room is visit is way more expensive than a regular doctor's visit. Then these people get the bills from the hospital but do not pay them because they can not afford to pay them. This causes the hospital to lose that money. Most hospitals are not non-profit organizations so the money they lose causes their service prices to be raised to offset the losses. Then once this is done the insurance companies that we all have for our health insurance sees costs going up from the hospital and in turn raise our insurance premiums. So, yes Mr. Insured American you are paying for all of these people that don't have health insurance in this country. So, why not make it easier on you and have it taken from your tax money? This way you will never have to worry about your health insurance going up or even hitting your ceiling on what the insurance company will pay. (My policy will pay a maximum of 1million dollars of benefits for me.) You will also not have to pay a deductible anymore and you will not have a copay either. See here is the problem we all want reform but we all say I don't want to have to pay for it. You might as well make it as fair for all as you can.

Here is how my plan works. Everyone in this country would be insured via the federal health care plan. We all would have to pay 5% of our gross income for this coverage. You make 100000 dollars a year you pay 5000. If you make 20000 dollars a year you pay 1000. Let us not forget the corporate hotshots here that are making millions, if you make 5 million per year you pay 250000 dollars for health coverage. We are all in this together. We all have the same exact coverage. We all have 100% coverage for all procedures and doctor visits. We all have no deductible. We all have no co-payment and we all have no worries about being able to afford a procedure that could save our lives. We also have no worries about our insurance saying no to these procedures. All required procedures would be covered. Not elective surgeries like boob jobs and nose jobs, just necessary ones.

This way the doctors have to deal with only one insurance plan and not 100's. This will help them cut overhead. Another good thing about this plan is that we the voters have a lot to say about our plan. It is one more issue for our politicians to talk about. If our quality of coverage slides our politicians are the ones that have to answer for it. In our current system we have people to call at our insurance companies but we never get to change the people running it. This way we do get to change them if we ever get ticked off for the quality of care going down.

Here is another story that will show the benefit of going to my federal health care plan. This is going to go back to my immigration chapter in this book but I think it needs to be said. You want health care in America you need to be a citizen. Period. End of story. My plan will require you to carry your federal health care plan card with you to get service and you will have to be subject to finger print verification. Yes, I am aware we all have situations where we lose our wallets, thus losing our cards, and that is what the finger print technology is for. We have the technology to track this info without the cards. Nobody's finger prints are the same as anyone else's finger prints. When this program goes into effect you have to go to the federal health care plan local office. (This also helps create local jobs) and apply for it and no legal citizen will be turned down (even if they are not working). You need to show proof of citizenship (birth certificate if you are a person born here or proof that you are a legal immigrant via following the proper legal channels.) As a part of this program we will need to start finger printing all people applying for the citizenship process. And the people that are born here would need to get fingerprinted at birth. That way from day one it would be in your local federal health care plan office. Anyone that does not have this ability would be sent to not for profit hospitals that are funded by grants and private funds. This would mean much less quality of care and longer wait times for services. And if you are an illegal immigrant, when physically able to be transported you would be sent back to the country from which you are from. Let's see how that country takes care of you. Do you think they will give you free health care? I highly doubt it!! (Unless you are from Canada) Again follow America's rules or GTFO!! Yes that is harsh, I know, but harsh times require harsh measures and I don't think it is fair that we are all paying for people that don't want to follow the rules and for people that don't pay taxes in this country.

Now as for the people that are unemployed and are unable to work because of disability or even the people that lose their jobs and have to stay unemployed because they can't find a job, they would still get this insurance and not have to worry about health care for themselves or their families. People that are able to work would have to attempt to get jobs and prove this to the federal health care local office. If you do not do this on a once a month basis you will be subject to the not for profit hospital. (By having the once a month requirement it keeps the local federal health care office people employed) Again harsh I know but we all work for a living and we are not here to support the people that don't want to take care of themselves. The people that are unable to take care of themselves I have no problem with. It is the people that are living off welfare and unemployment because they think it is easier than finding work and would rather not find a job because they don't feel that they have to because they can float on taxpayer money. That is going to stop!!

The beauty of this program is that we still get to choose our doctors and hospitals. We don't have to look through a book and find a new doctor because they will all be covered under this program.

I have heard some people say what about the people that work for these insurance companies and what about these insurance companies themselves? The people working for them can get jobs quite easily from the local federal health care program office. The health insurance companies on the other hand, well that is the downside. They will have to change their specialty. They can go into auto insurance, home insurance, and/or life insurance. You can't make an omelet without breaking a few eggs. These health insurance companies have been making a ton of money from all of us and they are part of the problem with our health care system and this is a solution. Sometimes we have to have things get worse before they get better and this will be better for all in the long run. Sorry insurance guys, I just call it like I see it.

I think I have posted a lot in this book about how we all need to make sacrifices and that includes doctors. Seeing how you will all be getting paid every single time no matter what, you need to cut your costs to the American public. You will assume no losses anymore.

You will assume no risk of not getting paid. So, time for you to make that sacrifice. Although like I said it really wouldn't be a sacrifice now would it. You will actually make more money under my plan. And that means you will be putting more money into it too.

Not saying this is the right way to do this, but I have a theory on how doctors and hospitals can get paid. The example I am going to use is my service department here at the dealership that I work for. They have a book that is used to figure out how they get paid by how many hours that job should take. For instance, let's say this book says that it takes 6 hours to install a transmission. That means my service department would get paid from the warranty company for 6 hours and 6 hours only. If our mechanic takes 7 hours to fix that transmission he only gets paid for the 6 hours. However if he gets the job done in 5 hours he still gets paid for 6 hours. Would I want my doctor trying to rush my surgery so he gets paid for a 6 hour surgery that only took him 5 hours, hell no!! But, I do believe doctors would not do that now that they are making all the money guaranteed. I believe our doctors would follow their Hippocratic oath and do what is best. But the more experienced doctors could do the job right and still get it done faster than a book time.

Each doctor will have to submit what they make per hour to the federal health care offices for approval. It will be at the federal governments discretion as to the approved upon hourly rate. This again will take in many factors. Some but not all of those factors are location, experience, or type of doctor (specialists, surgeons, or just general practitioners). The federal government could even set approved rates for hospitals and doctors based on location. Like I said earlier you need to figure for cost of living by location. Doctors in Manhattan and Los Angeles should make more than a guy in Podunk Arkansas. Doctors deserve a lot of money for what they do. They require a lot of extensive training and it is just plain gross sometimes. So they would deserve every cent they are charging. But they should not be allowed to just ravish the sick and take advantage of helpless people. And I do think that some of our doctors are doing that now because of the fact that there is no regulation on how much they can charge for their services.

One other idea that I have for doctors is a flat pay based on specialty. The brain surgeon would make 5 million dollars a year while the general practitioner would make 600,000 a year. And anything in between I could be way off on those numbers but you get the idea. If you set a figure based on the doctors specialty those doctors won't just live in areas where they can get paid the most. They will be readily available to anyone and everyone regardless of location. Can you imagine the positives of this? They would be endless. You have doctors living in smaller communities bringing up the value of homes. This would create a better community, and that would draw more businesses to that community, which would create more jobs in that community. See where I am going with this? It would benefit the doctors and everyone else in this country.

By enacting the federal health care program we can do all it takes to make sure that everyone is happy with the system. The people get the health care they desperately need. The doctors and hospitals get paid what they are owed and what they deserve. Everybody wins!!

I think I just knocked it out of the park with the federal health care program. But there is a whole other issue with health care that I have not touched on yet and that is medicine. Prescription drugs to be specific. I believe that our prescriptions should be covered under the federal health care program but with a slight twist. Read on.

It costs nearly 1 billion dollars to develop just one drug in this country. This is caused buy many factors starting with research and development. You have to have people developing the drugs and then testing them and that takes time and money. Believe it or not, R & D only accounts for a little less than half of the actual overall cost of the drug. The majority of the money spent on these drugs is the actual marketing of them. How many times have you turned on the television and you see a commercial for a new miracle drug that will cure something or mask the symptoms of something. Or the ever famous E.D. (erectile dis-function) drugs advertising segments? Well, that money comes from somewhere. They in turn pass that on to us the consumer. Oh, and what is up with the side effects of drugs today? Some of these side effects are worse than the illness that the drug is supposed to help.

For instance: do you suffer from watery eyes? Try "don't cry dry your eye" eye drops. And you will no longer have to worry about your eyes watering. Side effects include, itchy eyes, heart burn, nausea, anal leakage, rapid heart beat, high blood pressure, and diabetes. Who in their right mind would buy this? Probably nobody, but some of the drug commercials I see now are very similar to that farce that I came up with for watery eyes. It is just weird what people will buy. No matter what "it" is, I believe we will buy it as long as there is a commercial for it. (I think car manufacturers should have the following side effects for their cars...may cause you to get a speeding ticket, may cause death when mixed with other cars at high speeds, and vehicle may cause your bank account to shrink every month. Like I said before, I do crack myself up.)

Have you ever walked into a drug store or a pharmacy counter in a big superstore and take a look behind the pharmacy counter? They are just packed with filled prescriptions. I swear to all that is holy that 1 out of every 10 people in most towns has a prescription being filled every month. Month in and month out people need their prescriptions (and they always seem to be there when I need mine. Man those lines are long.) filled. There is a lot of money in prescription drugs even if it costs so much to develop. And drug company's do deserve to make some money for their brilliance and their hard work. However they need to realize, once and again, we are all in this together and they need to stop raping the American public.

So here is my drug plan. All drugs will be covered under the government health care plan but this time there will be a copay. You need to pay 20 for all name brand drugs and 10 dollars for all generic brands. I do not think what I am putting on here is a lot to ask for.

There are also going to have to be cost caps on these drugs. It is obvious to me that the drug companies are taking advantage of the need for the drugs. I just read where a prescription drug named Tamoxifen (a drug used to treat and prevent breast cancer...pretty important drug I think) costs over 100 dollars to fill at a Walgreens here in the United States but the same exact drug is available to Canadian people for only 10 dollars total. That is not a copay that is the total cost to the Canadian public. That is the same drug for 90% less. (Yes, I rounded the numbers.)

This is where Canada has it right with their medical plan. Their national price review board and their overall marketing power allows them to negotiate lower prices with the U.S. drug companies. In order to do business in Canada, U.S. drug companies do not add the cost of research and development and the price of lobbying and advertising costs to the drugs. So why does the drug company do it to Americans? Because they can. We don't have a national price review board. Whatever price the drug company sets is the price we pay because they don't have to answer to anyone. They don't have to answer to anyone except the American people and as long as we are willing to let them take our money they will.

I think that about covers a solution to the health care and prescription drug cost situation. What about our shortage of nurses?

Many people believe that nursing is the fastest growing need in the health care world. It is estimated that by the year 2025 we will have a shortage of 500,000 nurses.

In a statement released in March 2008, The Council on Physician and Nurse Supply, an independent group of health care leaders based at the University of Pennsylvania, has determined that 30,000 additional nurses should be graduated annually to meet the nation's health care needs, an expansion of 30% over the current number of annual nurse graduates.

With this kind of shortage happening, it is hard to believe that in the year 2007 it was reported that 147,000 qualified nursing candidates had to be turned down because the number of qualified nursing educators continues to drop. How can we let this happen? How can we turn people away in a job market that is actually growing in today's world? I mean come on, most of the job markets are shrinking and this one is growing but we are letting qualified people not get the training that they need.

My theory on the lack of nursing educators is that we are in such desperate need of nurses that the moment that a nurse graduates she wants to jump into work right away and get paid. To be a nursing educator you need your MSN. (And that has nothing to do with Microsoft). An MSN is a Master of Science in Nursing. So the nurse goes to school (providing she got accepted) and graduates in a field that needs her. She has a choice now of paying for more schooling and getting her masters in her field and then become an educator that doesn't pay as much as her actual job would. Wow tough choice there huh!! Keep in mind this is just a theory but that sure is what it sounds like is happening to me.

Right now we are importing nurses from all over the globe. We have nurses coming from the Philippines, China, Japan, Africa, and India. I am sure there are more than just these countries being used to bring nurses is but you get the point. Is this the answer to our nursing shortage? I think it could be part of the solution but not the main solution.

The main solution to this problem is we need to have a grant program set up for nurses to get their MSN. That way they don't have to pay for the extra schooling and many times these nurses can still work full time as a nurse and go to school at night or alternate times. We need to address this problem internally. We need to get our own people in nurses training. If you already have a nursing degree you should be able to get your MSN at no cost to you via this grant. That should take care of the instructor problem here. This solution that I have just proposed would not fix the problem right away but over time it would benefit our country in the long run.

Once again our system has it wrong. If we don't have enough people here to train our perspective candidates maybe that is who we should be importing. We should be bringing in the nursing trainers from these other countries and let them train the 147,000 people who want to be nurses in this country. We are bringing in thousands of nurses from these countries every year. How bout we actually get some nurses from these countries with their MSN already and hire them to train the people that actually want to do the job? Or how bout we set up a grant program for those people that want to be nurses to go to these countries to study. I am sure that some of these people would love to go abroad and study for the career they chose. Once again these answers might be too simple, but sometimes the simplest answers are truly the right ones.

Actually, the more I think about it, these may not be the best things to do. Like I stated earlier in this book how do we know what kind of training these nurses have? Are these nurses subject to the same testing in their home countries as they are here? When they come to this country are they being tested by our standards? I would say if the answers to these questions are yes, then I would be OK with it, but I don't know the answers to these questions. I certainly think that it should be required to pass the same tests our American trained nurses take.

A lot of the nurses are fed up with substandard working conditions. Some of my coworkers and I were just talking about some layoffs that happened at a local hospital. Then my boss brought up a fact where in some hospitals the cost cutting has gotten so bad that they are using 2 bedpans per floor and sharing. I will say eeeeeeeeeewwwwwwwwww to that!! That is just nasty. Is the all mighty dollar more important that someone's health and well being? Would you want your wife or husband to be in hospital where they can't afford a private bed pan, but they still charge you 600 a day to stay there?

Congratulations America you have just crossed a line that I hope we will cross back over soon. Anytime that we can honestly say to our people that money is more important than health, we know we are heading in the wrong direction. We need our government to step up and do what is right for all of us and our families. This is truly MESSED UP!!

What is being done to the American people when it comes to health care should be considered a crime.

Speaking of crimes...

CRIME AND PUNISHMENT

Our crimes here in America are getting out of control. White collar crimes or blue collar crimes it makes no difference. We have people ripping off people with guns and knives, and even pens and computers now days. We still have people killing people with guns and knives too. I am a firm believer that the punishment should be a deterrent for the crime that was committed. And I will supply some examples of what I mean.

I look at CNN.com all the time and see how this guy or that guy has taken millions of dollars from the company he worked for (and I am not just talking about CEO's and corporate big shots taking huge salaries here) or ripping off investors by running a scam or two.

Anyone reading this remember the Enron scandal? This was white collar crime at its finest. We are talking about a company that took itself down along with its accounting firm Arthur Anderson, which was at the time one of the five largest accounting firms in the world. For those of you that don't know about this or remember it, I will explain what Enron did. The company was reporting profits and revenue from deals with "special purpose entities" (limited partnerships which it controlled). The result of this was that a lot of Enron's debts and the losses that the corporation suffered were not reported on its financial statements. These so called special purpose entities were offshore corporations which were being used for planning and avoiding of taxes, thus raising the profitability of a the main business, Enron. By doing this, ownership and management was provided freedom to move the money around to and from these off shore corporations with full anonymity and keep the losses off the balance sheets of Enron. These offshore corporations made Enron look more profitable than it truly was. By showing billions of dollars of profit when in fact Enron was actually losing money, the stock of the company skyrocketed. Then the executives started to work on this inside information and started trading millions of dollars worth of Enron stock. You see, all the executive and insiders at Enron knew about these offshore corporations and the losses that they were hiding for Enron. However, the investors had no clue that this was happening. The CFO (chief financial officer) of Enron, Andrew Fastow was in charge of the team that created the off the book companies, and he is the one that manipulated deals to provide himself, his family, and his friends with hundreds of millions of dollars in guaranteed income, all of this at the expense of the corporation he worked for and its stock holders. (This information was paraphrased from Wikipedia.com)

So here is a guy that almost single-handedly brought down 2 humongous corporations. Costing thousands of jobs and millions of dollars to people who invested in these 2 companies. And what was his punishment? He got sentenced to 6 years in prison and 2 years of probation. I am sure that all the people that lost money because of him would agree that he got off quite easily. He had to forfeit 23.8 million dollars in family assets. But I am sure he has more than that stashed somewhere in other countries. When this jerk gets released in 2011 he will still be sitting pretty no matter where he goes. He will only be 50 years old and the people he screwed over will still be recovering from what he did. Here is a serious question for you. Would this a-hole be charged with murder if someone lost their whole life savings in Enron and decided to commit suicide because of it? Hell no he wouldn't. Another question I have is what happened to the 23.8 million that was seized? Were any of the people that lost money reimbursed anything from that 23.8 million dollars? I am sure it wasn't like the movie **THE JERK** starring Steve Martin, where he was writing the refund checks for the "optigrab" that caused all those problems for people and their eyes. I am willing to bet that our government kept this money and used it for something like a few really nice hammers and toilet seats.

I think this guy should be on probation until he makes restitution to all these people. He should have to work at any job he can get in the United States and 50% of his income should go to the fund for these people and their families. How is that for a deterrent for someone thinking of doing something like that?

Now we have Bernie Madoff running a multi-million dollar Ponzi scheme. In a Ponzi scheme investors are paid dividends from their own money. It is also known as a pyramid scheme. The person at the top collects more and more money from people below him. When this happens he sends money to the people below him from the people that are investing under them. For instance I start a corporation and I ask each investor to give me 10,000. I get 100 people to invest that. I now have 1 million dollars. Then I get 100 more people to invest 10,000 dollars again. But this time I take that million and give out 3000 to each of the first 100 people. So now I made another 700,000 dollars but the people that got on board first made 30% on their first investment. Then because the first set of people did so well on their investment that they tell others to join. Imagine this happening over and over and over again. Everyone underneath me is happy because they are making a lot of money off their initial investment. As long as new people keep investing the people that have already invested will keep making money. It is when new people stop investing or the people already invested stop throwing money in that it all falls down like a house of cards. No more money coming in means no more going out. Then all the investors want out and BOOM!! It is over.

Mr. Madoff is out on 10 million dollars bail and if convicted the max he would receive is 20 years of prison and a fine of 5 million dollars. . This is a guy that was chairman of the NASDAQ stock exchange. He opened his company (Bernard L. Madoff Investment Securities LLC) in 1960 and was the chairman of that corporation until December 11, 2008 when he was charged with investor fraud/securities fraud. He was a highly respected businessman in our country and a whole lot of people trusted this man with a lot, if not all, of their money. And the most he could do is 20 years and pay 5 million dollars? Pardon me but what the hell!! Again this punishment doesn't fit his crime. Come on, this guy is 70 years old. He lived high on the hog from his Ponzi scheme investors for as many as 48 years and I am sure he has stashed money all over the world so his family is taken care of after he is in prison or even after he dies.

How can we let this happen? What can we do to help the people out that lost some or all of their money? I say what needs to be done is actually investigate all of his financial transactions over the last 48 years. Find out where all of the money from his corporation went to. I am sure he has off shore accounts opened up somewhere. I know his son's will help find it. They are the ones that turned him in!! Big OUCH!! His own son's turned him in on securities fraud. Even they know what is right and wrong. Good for them. (I wonder if they get a reward?)

Here is a personal story that has to go along with crime and punishment. I was working at a dealership and the GM there was doing all sorts of illegal activities involving the Internet. This man created a website that was only accessible via being a member. On this website were movies that were not even out at theaters yet. Remember the movie THE PASSION OF THE CHRIST? This man had it on DVD before it was even released to the movie theaters. I know this because he gave me a copy of it. (Yep you guessed it that made me an accessory.) Also on this website were video games, other movies that were out but still were copyrighted, programs like Microsoft office, and even corporate programs. He once told me that the reason he was doing this wasn't because of the membership money he was charging for the memberships it was because of the fact he could do it and not get caught. Well he did get caught and let me tell you how he got caught. ME!! That's right; I turned him in to the FBI. Keep reading and I will explain the whole story.

My General Manager was a true computer genius. He built computers and fixed computers. If ever there was something wrong with a computer this man could fix it. I am pretty sure there was nothing he couldn't do with a computer. So anywho, I had a problem with my cheap ass computer and brought it to him to fix it. He wound up rebuilding it making it faster and more memory. All he asked me to do was pay for the hardware and he would take care of all the software that I would need. Not a bad deal for me at all.

One week later I got my computer back with all the programs I would ever need to use. I am talking windows, Microsoft office, excel, you name it I had it. I also had an interesting little shortcut I have never seen before. This shortcut was the shortcut to my GM's website. He then gave me my own password and said if I ever find a program I wanted to just tell him and he will post it on his website and I can have it for free. I asked him if I needed to pay his membership fee for the website and he said don't worry about it.

Here I was sitting with access to any movie I wanted, any program I needed, and just about anything I needed for my computer at my fingertips anytime I wanted them. Unfortunately for my boss, I had a conscience. I was having a hard time sleeping at night knowing that

I was involved in some major crimes happening here. I mean copyright infringement, Internet fraud, and just plain theft to name just a few. This was really starting to eat at me. One day as I was driving home I started thinking what could happen to me if I got caught with all this illegal stuff on my computer. I had a wife and kids to think about. So now it was not only my conscience eating at me, it was my family's well being. It was right then in the car ride home that I called the FBI and talked to one of the agents in the computer fraud division. He didn't seem to care at all about what I was telling him. He took my information and said he will check it out. I thought that would be the last I heard of it and didn't care anymore because my conscience was clear, knowing I did the right thing.

Two weeks later I get a call from the FBI agent I spoke to and he wants to meet with me the following day for lunch. No problem I figured at the very least I would get a free lunch on the government. We met and he started asking me what movies were on the website and if I could get him access to the site. I told him no problem and we agreed to have him come to my house and look at the website from my computer. That way there would be no suspicion on my boss's part.

The FBI came to the house on my day off and took a look at what was on his website. We went through all the movies, then the games, then the big one...the programs. They were astonished to find a program on his site that had a value of over 25,000 dollars. This particular program ran a whole corporation. It was designed for the purpose of running multi million dollar corporations and they only knew of one company using it. I guess that

I had their attention now because they wanted to come back the following week and bring a portable hard drive so they could copy some of the smaller programs to this hard drive.

This procedure went on for about a month. They would come over on my day off and download programs, games, and movies to this hard drive. Week after week my boss had more and more things on his website. It was getting bigger by the day. More movies, more games, and more programs. Then after about a month they went for it. They started downloading the 25,000 dollar program. It took almost 6 full hours to download to the hard drive. The FBI agents (now there were 2 of them) told me that would be all they needed from me and they would keep me informed about what was happening with the case as time went on. They also let me know that I should keep right on doing what I was doing. Downloading games, programs, and movies as to not arise any suspicions.

It was over a year and a half before I heard anymore from these guys, then one day they called my cell phone and let me know that they would be arresting him the following morning and doing a full blown raid on his house. I was told to just go to work like normal. (I figured that was easy considering I didn't work for him anymore...lol) They later called me up and told me that it went uneventful and he was in custody. In his house he had 3 servers running and they estimated he had over 2 million dollars worth of programs, video games, and movies on his computer. They also mentioned that if I should receive a phone call or email from him to notify them immediately. Even though they never told him who it was that turned him in he may be able to figure it out based on the evidence presented. (And if he buys this book I am sure he will know now.)

Now here is the weird part. It took two whole years to get him convicted and take a wild guess what he got? A 200,000 dollar fine, 3 years probation, and 6 month's of house arrest. This is getting out of hand I think. This guy was stealing millions of dollars worth of programs, games, and movies and he gets a low ass sentence like that.

It seems to me that crime is getting worse and worse every year. But the punishments are getting softer and softer. One of the crimes I am seeing happen more and more is a mother killing her own kids. It is like these women see another woman that did it on TV and realize it is the way for them to go. I am a father of 4 kids, and although I have gotten really upset with them, the thought of killing them has never ever crossed my mind. Yet for these women it is one of the first things they think of. How in the hell is that even a rational thought?

In 2001 Andrea Yates drowned her five kids ranging in ages 7years to 6 months old. While she was drowning her youngest baby her oldest son asked what is wrong with Mary. She proceeded to chase him throughout the house until she caught him and drowned him as well. In 2002 she was found guilty of capital murder and was sentenced to life in prison. In 2006 however that ruling was overturned and she was acquitted of capital murder by reason of insanity. She is still in custody but now she is in a psychiatric hospital and they firmly believe she will never get out.

In 2008 Leatrice Brewer drowned her 3 kids and laid their wet bodies side by side on her bed before drinking a drink consisting of bleach, cleaning chemicals and aspirin. She woke up 4 hours later, and after realizing she was still alive, she called 911 to tell them what she had done. Then she proceeded to jump out of a second-story window in a second suicide attempt. Leatrice has not been sentenced as of February 2009, but on February 9, 2009 she did plead not guilty by reason of insanity.

If these women are truly insane and unable to live normal lives I say here is what we do. We take both of these women and put them in a cage. We sink said cage into a pool. We watch them drown. We record it and maybe even televise it. Once these women drown we bring them out and revive them. Make sure they get nice and clear headed again and then we say "That is what you put your innocent little children through. How did that feel?" Then we let them sit on death row for a year to think about it and remember that experience. Then 1 year later we do it again only this time we don't bring them back. We let them die knowing what they did and living through the anguish of what they did to their children and how they felt. I want them to go to hell remembering what their children had gone through. If these women are truly not mentally capable of understanding what they did then they won't understand what is happening to them. But it sure will be a deterrent for those other women out there that think they can kill their kids and plead insanity so they don't have to die. Even the really mentally ill women will think twice after watching these women go through their ordeal. Women like Casey Anthony, who is currently accused of killing her 2 year old daughter Caylee Marie. Maybe if she would have seen a woman get executed for killing their kids little Caylee would still be alive today. We will never know because we care more about the people that commit the crime as opposed to the people who have had the crime committed against them.

Our criminal justice system is so MESSED UP. It seems as though the criminals are the only ones getting justice. Maybe we should call it the justice for criminals system. Want more proof? I will give it to you. O.J. Simpson...just kidding, I have more than that. I think the O.J. horse has been beaten to death, no pun intended and O.J. belongs in the next chapter not this one.

On March 22, 2006 Mary Winkler shot her minister husband Matthew Winkler in the back while he was lying in bed. She then ran away with their 3 kids of 8 and 6 years old, and the 1 year old baby. His body was discovered by people that went to his home to check on him after he didn't show up for that night's services. The police had thought that Mary and her children may have been kidnapped so they sent out an amber alert. They were found in Orange Beach, Alabama. When she was asked by investigators what happened to her husband, Winkler stated that her and her husband had argued about money and offered "I guess that is when my ugly came out." On June 12, 2006 a grand jury indicted Mary Winkler, accusing her of first degree murder.

In the statement she gave to Alabama authorities she says she didn't remember getting the gun but she did know her husband kept a shotgun in their home. The next thing she heard was a loud boom. Her husband was shot in the back as he lay in bed. He rolled onto the floor, and, still alive he asked his wife of 10 years "Why?" to which she responded " I'm sorry." When she left their home he was still alive in the bedroom, and the phone had been disconnected from the wall socket.

On April 18,2007 Mary took the stand in her own defense. Mary told the jury that her husband often "berated" her and forced her to wear "slutty" costumes for sex. She even supplied a pair of high-heeled shoes and a wig to use as proof, and the people in the courtroom gasped. She claimed that she only shot her husband by accident. She said that she went for the gun because she wanted to force him to "work through their problems." She then stated "I just wanted him to stop being so mean." Mary later claimed that she never pulled the trigger, but told the jury "something went off." She heard a boom, then ran from the house because she thought he would be mad at her. She also said "He had really been on me lately, criticizing me for things- the way I walk, I eat, everything. It was just building up to a point. I was tired of it. I guess I got to a point and snapped."

I am going to dissect this ridiculous story for a minute here. I know if I had seen my wife with a gun aimed at me I would have worked through anything she wanted. No ifs ands or buts about it. But that is the key. He was lying on his stomach, he couldn't see her. If she truly did it by accident, he would have been lying on his back at the very least and talking to him. She never pulled the trigger? Something went off? She just heard a boom? I personally have shot a 12 gauge shotgun and first off it takes some effort to pull the trigger. Secondly, if that gun was near you it would not sound like "something went off", it would sound like a bomb went off in front of you. Thirdly, she would not have just heard a boom. Again it would have been very loud and that gun has quite a kick. It probably would have knocked her on her ass!! At the very least it would have flown out of her hands. She was out and out lying!! The only truth she told was about her snapping. You are right Mary; you snapped and killed your husband.

Here is the real problem that comes in. On April 19, 2007, the jury came back with a verdict: guilty of voluntary manslaughter. (Voluntary manslaughter is the killing of a human being in which the offender had no prior intent to kill and acted during "the heat of passion", under the circumstances that would cause a reasonable person to become emotionally or mentally disturbed.... [thank you again wikipediafor a great definition]) The prosecutors were asking for her to be convicted of first-degree murder, but after only 8 hours of deliberation they decided on the lesser charge. I do not condone a person "berating" another person but I firmly believe Mary was not in the heat of passion at that moment. He may have ticked her off earlier but it wasn't right at that moment. I mean come one people, her husband was lying on his stomach. He wasn't in her face. He wasn't sitting up. He wasn't hitting her. He was lying on his stomach not charging at her. He was completely defenseless. I believe she acted in cold blood and was lying her ass off to get the lesser sentence.

Her sentencing was even more MESSED UP. On June 8, 2007, a Tennessee judge sentenced Mary Winkler to 210 days in prison for the conviction of voluntary manslaughter. She has credit for already serving 5 months and the judge permitted her to spend up to 60 days in a Western State Mental Health Facility in Bolivar, Tennessee. That will be all the time she has remaining. She will then be put on probation for the rest of her sentence. You have got to be kidding me. 5 months in prison, 60 days in a mental facility, and then probation for like what, a week? This woman is a cold blooded killer. I don't care if her husband was making her swallow quarters and crap out nickels. I don't care if he called her every name in the book in front of her mother, the man didn't deserve to die. He may have deserved to be divorced because of that, but certainly not dead. This lady herself appeared on Oprah recently and even she thinks she got off too easy. My god this woman even got full custody of her kids after all this. How the hell is this possible? HELLO??? She killed their daddy!!! Who was smoking the wacky tobacky that day?

Here is one more personal experience that has to do with crime and punishment. This one involves my first ex wife. I told you I had 2 of them. This particular one went nuts. Not in terms of "oh man my wife went nuts on me..." as a euphemism. I mean "we the jury find the defendant as..." Boy oh boy, I wish I was making that up. My ex wife spent 2 years in prison. 2 years of a 4 year sentence. Man oh man, you got to read this, it is a good one...

We had been married for 7 years and my wife was working for a local company as an office manager. We had been doing pretty well I was making a good living as a finance manager for a small dealership and as an office manager she was making a decent living.

Then one day she told me she got a promotion. She was now earning commission on selling machines for her company. I thought cool and good for her. It was at this point money started rolling in. She was bringing in almost as much as I was. She was spending it as fast as she could make it, too. She bought a pool for the backyard. Not one of those blow up ones either. She bought a 30 foot by 23 foot oval pool that was half in ground and half out of the ground. She bought a 12000 dollar deck for the pool. Then to top off the deck she bought a hot tub for it.

Who was I to question anything? I mean I am in commission sales and the more I sold the more I got paid, so I can see how she could be making a lot more money based on this. She was in control of our finances and we were doing good. All of our bills were paid. I was able to sock some money away in the bank and also in my company's 401k plan. Like I said, times were good.

Then the big bomb! One day I was at work and got a call from my wife's boss. He told me that he had to let her go today and that she was very upset and he even thought she might be suicidal. I kept asking him what the hell happened and he wouldn't give me an answer. I proceeded to ask "I thought she just got a promotion and was doing well. How can you let a person go that was doing so well?" He said "You really don't know what is going on? I will have to let her tell you then. I just suggest that you call her right away so she doesn't do anything stupid." I did call her right away and she told me she is fine and that we needed to talk.

I got home that night and she proceeded to tell me how she had been embezzling money from the company she was working for and that this money is what she had been spending. She told me how she opened up an account at a nearby bank in her company's name with her listed as the only signer. She then proceeded to deposit all incoming checks to the company she worked for into this account. Why would the bank question anything at all. She had all the proper paperwork and tax ID numbers so they kept taking checks from her and depositing into her bogus account. She kept spending and spending. She was making daily trips to the local WalMart for herself and the kid's clothes. By the time she was caught she had taken a total of 125,000 dollars from her employer.

Needless to say I flipped out! I told her I was done. I couldn't trust her anymore and she needed to get out. And get away from me and the kids as soon as possible. Here was a woman I thought I knew. I did still love her but I couldn't look her in the eye wondering if what she told me was a lie or the truth anymore. So, I gave her some money so she wasn't homeless and the next day she found an apartment a few blocks from the house so she could still be near the kids.

She started taking small jobs like catering waitress, cook, etc. Pretty much anything to do with food service. She couldn't do anything that involved money or she probably would have stolen it. She was doing all she could to make a living while I kept distancing myself from her.

One day when she came over to get the kids so they could spend time with her, the police pulled up and arrested her. Finally I thought. The bad thing was that it happened right in front of my 2 kids. The kids were 7 and 6 and all they saw was mommy crying and being taken away kicking and screaming. They took her downtown and booked her. She wound up calling one of her friends to come up with her 1000 bail. Her actual bail was 10,000 but in Illinois you only need 10 percent to get out. That friend called me and asked me for the money, but of course I didn't give it up. I figured that jail was the best place for her at this point. The kids didn't need to be involved any more than they already were. I don't know how this friend came up with the money but a couple days later my wife was out of jail and back to making me nuts.

A few days after her arrest was when it got nuts for me. I was out playing golf with one of my friends on my day off, the kids were in school, and my mom stopped by to let the dogs out when the sheriff showed up with papers to seize my house, cars, and every single possession I had. The claim was that everything was bought with this ill gotten money and that I was a conspirator of the whole thing. I found out later that my wife actually told the police the opposite. She told them I had nothing to do with it and that I didn't even know anything about what she had done.

It was 3 days later I was able to get back into my home and live there until the court system determined the houses fate. Like I told you earlier they seized my cars and even my motor cycle. I owned the motorcycle outright but the cars had loans on them and they had no right to them by law. But apparently in Illinois that particular law didn't mean jack shit because they kept these things for 3 years while I continued to make payments on them and fought to get them back.

It took 2 years because my wife kept postponing her trial because she kept bouncing checks to her attorney's. She must have gone through 5 defense attorneys before her sentencing was final. When all was said and done she was sentenced to 4 years hard time. With time off for good behavior it was cut to 2 years. The kicker was that I had to still fight to get my belongings back and to get a lien taken off my house that was put on it from the company she stole from.

If you notice it took 2 years to get her sentenced but I listed above that it took me 3 years to get my cars back. (4 years for the motorcycle) The only reason I was able to get my cars back is I finally decided that I will stop paying on them and let the banks repossess them. What the hell did I care I wasn't able to use them anyway. Once they called me and told me I owed them money and I was behind with them I told them the whole story and they immediately got them back and I redeemed them by catching up on the late payments. They were very forgiving considering that I paid on them for 3 years without having them. (If only the mortgage companies that hold the mortgages for the people behind today would be as forgiving.) As for the lien on the house that was never removed and I let the bank take that house and let her former employer deal with getting money from the mortgage holder. With that lien on there I couldn't refinance the house, I couldn't sell the house, I couldn't do a darn thing with it. The lien was for 100,000 dollars. Tack that on to my mortgage and it just wasn't worth fighting anymore. So I let the bank foreclose and I had no more worries about the lien.

She got 2 years of prison for completely destroying a company. Do you think that was fair? Not only did she only get 2 years, she also didn't have to pay any of the money back that she stole. Granted, at the time she was arrested they did seize the account she had opened up. In that account was 50,000 dollars approximately. So that company lost 75,000 dollars and because of the loss of money and time had to close the doors to the company. They just couldn't absorb that kind of loss in that short period of time.

I think that she should have had to pay it all back with interest!! That way the people would have been able to get back on their feet.

I did get one thing out of all this. While she was in jail our divorce was finalized and I got sole custody of our kids.

Now that I am talking about custody and divorce...

DATING/MARRIAGE/ DIVORCE

The American family is in danger and has been for a very long time. Statistics right now show that over 50% of all marriages end in divorce. I am speaking from a lot of experience here. I have been divorced twice and let me tell you it is no fun. In this chapter I will be pointing out some very important facts about dating,marriage, and divorce. If you have ever been divorced, keep reading. If you are thinking about getting a divorce, keep reading. If you are thinking about getting married, keep reading. If you are dating, keep reading. If you are thinking you are never getting married, even you should keep reading. This chapter is chocked full of information for everyone.

A lot of you are all probably asking why I would put this chapter in a book about politics, government, and things of that nature. I don't blame you for asking that at all. But let me explain. I am not just talking about our government and the problems they create. I am talking in this book about how MESSED UP all of America is. And one of the problems in our country right now is the loss of the true family life. Dating, marriage, and divorce have a lot to do with that.

I am going to start with dating. Dating is the first step in getting a significant other. You have to start somewhere and this is it. I have learned there are three things a man needs in life. Food, sleep, and sex. So for women it is pretty easy. Once you have a guy if he gets those 3 things with you he will be happy. Women have 4 things they need. Conversation/communication, honesty,security, and compassion. (See women always want more than men do...lol!!)If a woman finds these four qualities in a man she will be happy. If these things are met for both parties at the same exact time you have a great match and a long lasting relationship.

Now, to start dating you have to meet someone. Then you have to get him or her to go on that date. Easy right? Wrong. In today's world there are so many obstacles to dating. I will touch on some of those, and you will see how they tie in with the rest of the book.

One of the problems in today's dating world is that sexual harassment exists. When sexual harassment was first becoming a household word I was about 17 years old and I was watching the TV with my grandfather who was 88 at the time. A news report came on that said a woman who was harassed at her job by a co-worker is suing because it made her uncomfortable. At this exact moment my grandfather busted out laughing. So of course I asked him why. He said and I quote "if it wasn't for sexual harassment I would have never gotten a date with your grandmother." He told me that my grandmother turned him down 4 times before she said yes to a date. Now days, that would be considered stalking. That story by my grandfather has stuck in my head a lot as an adult. In today's world if you go up to a woman you work with and do any flirting, she could take that as sexual harassment and boom you are out of a job, or worse, you get sued and lose your job at the same time. OK, so work is out as a place to meet your significant other. Unless she approaches you first, then it could be on, but you still have to be very careful. (I say she, but it could be a he too, like in the movie DISCLOSURE as I pointed out earlier.) Think before you act is what it comes down to. In today's economy, if you lose your job you may not get another one. In that case I wish you luck. No job equals no love.

And that brings me to economic situations. Even if you are working, you may just be making ends meet. So how can you afford to take a woman (or man)out on the town? How can you afford to wine and dine? Some average Joes or Josephines may actually have a hard time doing things that go along with traditional dating. A movie at my local theater is $8.50 per person and then there is popcorn, candy, and something to drink. You are looking at a movie date as about 50 dollars. Let's not forget dinner first. Unless you never want to see your date again, you are not going to take her to a fast food restaurant. An average to nice dinner is going to cost you at least 50 dollars. A really nice dinner is going to cost you 100-200 dollars. I save those until we have been dating a long time. I am not going to try and buy a woman. I want her to know me for me, not the money I have. Call me cheap if you want, but that is a lot of money for a first date and that is why I save it until later on.

This is why on line dating is so huge. You get to know a person before you meet up. You get to ask them anything and everything. Then your first date is just about actually making sure the person is who they say they are and they have all the right equipment in the right place, so to speak. This also cuts costs down a lot.

Sites like Eharmony, Match, and Chemistry all charge a monthly fee for you to meet people of the opposite sex. Eharmony and Chemistry pick the people out for you based on a series of questions you are asked when you sign up. Then once you are matched you read their profile and determine if you want to proceed. If you do you send that person a series of questions and if they are equally interested in you they answer them. If they are not they close you out and move on. Match on the other hand has you fill out your profile and you are free to go look for your match based on how they filled out their profiles. I have been a member of each of these and I can say there is not much difference in how it goes. You still have to find someone that is equally interested in you and go through all you normally would when you meet someone new. The biggest difference here is that it is only costing you the monthly fee to find them. And when you finally do meet them you already have gotten past the awkward stage. I have 2 people I know that have met their fiancé's via on line dating. No, it isn't right for everyone, but it is possible to meet the perfect person on line.

In my 37 years of existence I have been on my fair share of dates. I have been on good ones and some real humdingers!! There have been women that have outright lied on their on line profiles. And then there have been women that have told the truth about most things but when we met up they acted totally different. I will now tell you some of those "interesting" dating stories.

I started talking to this woman via an on line dating service. We seemed to have hit it off personality wise. She did not have a picture posted on the website, but I decided this time I was going to be concerned with how the woman was as opposed to just how she looked. She did describe herself as attractive with an average body. I wanted more in a woman than how she looked, so the picture didn't matter to me. Yes, physical attraction is important, but in the long run looks will fade and you are still going to be with this person, so you have to have a lot more than just sex and good looks working for you. So, anyway, we talked on line for a few weeks and then decided we would talk on the phone. Her voice was awesome and I liked what she had to say and how she said it. Here is the thing, I am an in-your-face kind of guy. I will make some off color jokes and talk about things a lot of people wouldn't dare speak of. This woman took me as who I was and didn't judge me or my open attitude. We got along great. So after a few days of talking we decided to meet up. I was excited. It was going to be a Saturday night I was going to pick her up at her place and we were going to go to dinner and maybe a movie. It worked out nicely because my 2 older kids were going to see a movie at a different theater with their friends and I didn't want to see that particular movie.

I worked until 5 pm that night and was on my way to pick her up. Still excited, I was getting directions from her on the phone and we talked about what we were going to do and where we were going to go. I got to her apartment and she met me at the door. I am very glad at this point that I do what I do for a living because I see all kinds of people. Let me tell you this lady was not of average body. She was not anything like she described. I know you are probably saying "so what? You liked her personality you should give her a chance." Well I didn't. Call me superficial if you must but you don't understand. Average body to me is a woman that is not super thin and is not super fat. Well this particular woman was at least 300 pounds. As for her face it might have been beautiful but I couldn't see it because it was all scrunched up from the fat in her face. I don't even know how she opened her eyes to see out of them. Now, I am not a total jerk, I was still willing to go out with her and take her to dinner. But once inside of her apartment, she started making passes at me that I was no longer comfortable with. I asked her where her computer was so I could look up the movie times again. While I did this I also texted my 16 year old son's cell phone with this message, "CALL ME NOW!!" He responded with "Why, what did I do?" I sent the same message again to him. He sent back the same response again. I sent him "just do it now!!" I made sure my ringer was on full blast as he called. I answered the phone and started yelling at him. Telling him if he didn't stop I would take away his cell phone and ground him for 2 weeks. I told him that I have had enough and was on my way home. The whole time I am doing this my son is getting upset and saying "what the heck are you talking about?" I hung up the phone and told this woman I had to leave my son was acting up with his grandmother and I had to go get him. I gave her a hug and said talk to you later. I never did call her again. I did, however, call my son right back and apologize to him and told him the story and he busted out laughing. I am sure a lot of you reading this think I am a jerk because of the fact that I didn't give her a chance because of how she looked. Well that was only part of the reason I didn't give her a chance. I didn't give her a chance because of that and the fact that she lied to me. Had she told me something like "I am a larger woman" upfront I still may not have given her a chance, but I would have at least respected her honesty. We will never know if I would have because she didn't tell me the truth.

There is another horror dating story I have. Sure, it started out good enough, but it didn't work out in the long run. We met via one of the dating sites and once again we hit it off right away. We had almost everything in common. We like the same movies, we liked the same food, and we were attracted to each other. This particular woman didn't have her picture posted either but she said it was because she didn't know how to put it on the site. She did however send me a picture from her cell phone and even though it was blurry I could tell she wasn't lying when she said she was good looking. We agreed to meet up at one of my favorite restaurants for lunch. It was the perfect lunch. We talked and talked and talked for what seemed like only a few minutes but it was actually 2 hours. I had to go and we agreed to see each other again. We did see each other again and again and again.

Pretty soon we were doing almost everything together. We would take my kids and her daughter to the zoo. We went to the children's museum. We literally were doing almost everything together. We must have spoken on the phone 10 times a day. She was the last voice I heard before I went to bed and she was the first voice I heard when I woke up. I was enjoying every minute with her and it seemed like she was enjoying every minute with me. And then it happened.

Her ex husband found out about me. He went nuts on her in front of her daughter on the day before mother's day of all days. First off let me tell you about this guy. This guy would not show up to pick up his daughter on the weekends he was supposed to, and he would bring her back early on the weekends he actually did pick her up. When their daughter was there he wouldn't do anything special with her he would just sit and drink and play his guitar hero video game. He was not reliable at all and certainly wasn't a good father. Not to mention they had been divorced for a few years already, and she had dated other guys before me. But he flipped out because we were getting very close. She called me that day to cancel our plans because he was yelling at her and she had to get her daughter. I said I understand and will be here if she needs anything from me. Just to talk or even come get her if she needs help. I should have told you this earlier but he was about 6'3" tall and about 270 pounds. The girl I was seeing was 4'10" tall and about 110 pounds. So needless to say I was concerned about her safety. I called her a few times that night but didn't get a response. The last message I left her was to just call me and tell me she was OK. Still nothing. The next day was mothers day. I wanted to take her out for a pleasant mother's day brunch or lunch because in the 5 years she had been a mother she never had a good mother's day. They had always been crappy and something always screwed it up for her. Needless to say I wanted this day to be special for her. So I called her cell phone and she still didn't answer it. So I left another message. No response. I waited about an hour and called again. She finally answered this time and proceeded to yell at me and saying I was stalking her and I should leave her alone. Did I do something wrong here? I don't think so. We wound up speaking the next day and she said we should slow down and explained that her ex yelled at her on the phone and when she got there he proceeded to yell at her in front of her daughter. She left there in tears and didn't want to talk about it. The next day she went to lunch with one of her friends instead of me because she was thinking I was pushing too hard. Based on that situation I came to the conclusion that she was more concerned with how her ex husband acted toward her than how I felt. It all went down hill from there.

We wound up giving it another shot a few months after we broke up but the same stuff kept happening. We would have plans and he would cancel the weekend he was supposed to have his daughter so we canceled our plans. I told her that is fine we just need to change our plans. I mean her daughter got along with me and my kids and we all got along together so bring her daughter along and we could all hang out and do something. She said that she just wanted to spend it with her daughter now. So I gave up on her after about the 4th time that happened.

Another interesting thing about her was that she was very giving. She was giving to all her friends. She was always there for them. The friend she went to mother's day lunch with was actually living in her house and mooching everything off of her. She would leave her son with my girlfriend and say she was going to run errands and not show up until the middle of the night, like 2 or 3 am. She would not pay for anything in the house. She wouldn't contribute to any part of the house because she couldn't afford to. I remember one time her gas got shut off because she didn't pay the bill and I told her she could wash clothes at my house and she could also take a shower at my house if need be and so could her daughter. But she once again didn't want her ex to find out about her daughter taking a shower at my house.

Just to give you an idea of how MESSED UP the people in her life are I am going to tell you another story about her friend, the mooch, and her ex husband. After the mooch left her house she moved into a government assisted facility that my ex girlfriend got for her. It was not far from where my ex girlfriend's ex husband lived. This turned out even more weird after she moved there because now the mooch and the ex husband are dating. Yep you read it right. The two people she chose over me are now together. And how did she find this out you may ask? Her ex husband hasn't paid child support in 5 months and he found out she got a big tax return. So he told her that he was going to be evicted from his apartment. He told her this on the weekend he was supposed to have his daughter. He promised to take his daughter to a monster truck show that weekend but he said he couldn't afford it. My ex girlfriend decided she didn't want her daughter to be disappointed so she offered to buy the tickets for them to go and she even offered to pay his rent up to date. He never told her how much the rent was so she didn't pay it and she didn't buy the truck tickets either. She did however buy groceries for her ex and their daughter so they could have food to eat for the weekend. Talk about mooching...wow! That night he did wind up taking their daughter and her mooch friend and the mooches son to the monster truck rally. Talk about just totally sticking it to his ex. The two people that caused us to not be together are now together and rubbing her nose in it and still mooching off of her together. That is truly MESSED UP!!

Here is yet another example of this woman and who she chooses to be with. My ex girlfriend had a "best" friend that used her too. This woman would drink and get hammered and my girlfriend would have to go pick her up so she would make it home safely. There was one time her friend and her husband were drinking beers in front of the place where their 2 daughters were dancing and exercising and the lady's daughters called my girlfriend to come pick them up and when she got there she saw at least 20 empty beer cans on the ground and in the car. Between the mooch who lived in her house and the friend that was constantly drunk and needing her she had zero time for me and she couldn't make time because of her ex husband. It was like this woman had such low self esteem that she had to please these people that used her and abused her. But someone (a.k.a. me) that showed her how she deserved to be treated and actually treated her very well she couldn't deal with it and pushed that person (again a.k.a. me) away because she didn't think she deserved it and was afraid of it.

This same woman now contacts me at least once a month for one thing or another. One month it might be car trouble and another month it will be something like how did my kids enjoy the Christmas gifts I got them. It literally is something different every time. I am nice every time she calls and try to help her with whatever she needs but I try not to be too personally involved with her because I am not going to go down that road again without some kind of proof she would treat me differently. I told her quite a while ago that if she wanted to get back with me let me know and if I am available I might consider it. And I would, if I am not already with someone, and that is a big if. I truly did fall in love with this woman in a very short period of time and she loved me. I knew she did even though we never said it to each other. I could tell and I know she knew how I felt. I was in love with her and her daughter as well. I would have done anything for them. That is what love is. But I learned that I wanted more than she could give and frankly I deserved more than she would give. As with most of you I want a person that puts my needs above an ex's needs and wants. If you truly love someone or even care about them you should be able to defend your relationship to an ex or anyone for that matter with ease. Maybe she just used this as an excuse because she was scared. I may never ever know. It is a shame we were compatible in every way and we would have been great together but it was just another dating nightmare for me.

Here is another story about dating, but it is not about me. It is about a friend of mine. And it is a female friend at that. This very nice young lady has been dating her boyfriend for 2 years. She seems happy with him but he is non-committal. He tells her he loves her but won't commit to her. Sounds like a lot of men out there doesn't it? Now here is the real kicker. One of my other female friends just got engaged to her boyfriend after dating just one year. I should also mention that both of these women are friends also. (This woman got engaged to another one of my friends and let me tell you this, they are a great couple. They truly fit together perfectly.) My other coworker who is not engaged went to her boyfriend and talked to him about this and said how weird it was that they have been dating twice as long as her friends and they are engaged and but she isn't.

His response is what is the most interesting to me. He said that he wanted to save up enough money for the wedding. He wanted her to have the best of the best and for money to be no object. He wanted her to be able to go to him and say I want this thing for the wedding and he would be able to get it for her without any restraint. BULLSHIT!!! To be engaged all you need is love and a ring for your fiancé. If love is there, and you truly want to be with her for the rest of your life, and she is in love with you, it wouldn't matter if you were married for 200 bucks by a fake fat Elvis in Las Vegas or if you are married in Italy at the Vatican by the Pope himself. All that matters is that you are going to be together forever. I know my friend pretty well (I don't know her boyfriend at all) and she isn't concerned about money or what she can and can not do at her wedding. She wants to be in a relationship that is going somewhere. This woman has a daughter and is living with her parents. She wants to be a wife, a mother, and most importantly she wants an American family. She wants the house, the white picket fence, the 2.3 kids, the dog, the whole nine yards. And this guy is just jerking her around. She tells me that she doesn't want to throw 2 years of her life away. She thinks he will eventually come around and want the same things she does. He is not the mature person that she needs him to be. But she needs to really sit this guy down and basically put it on the line for him. "It has been 2 years, your free trial is up. Either buy it or return it so someone else can treat it like it should be treated!!" And let me tell you this woman deserves to be treated well. And with her fantastic personality and physical appearance she could land any man she wants. The problem is she wants the man she has and he just wants to be a kid and not be a man.

This is the problem with dating. You find the one you want and they don't want you. The good ones you find are already taken. The ones you do find have a past relationship that is so haunting to them that they decide to take a break from dating. Lets face it everyone out in the dating world has a past or a present that is not good. If they didn't have a weird past or weird situation presently they would be married already. We just have to figure out what is acceptable to us and what is not acceptable to us. Once we do that we will find it is a lot easier to find the person that will want to be with us and the one that we want to be with.

Those are just a few of the bad dating stories I know. Obviously there have been good dating stories. If there were no good stories nobody would be married. However, this book isn't about those stories. This book is about things being MESSED UP. Not being happy. If you paid attention during my media chapter you would remember that I said good news doesn't sell. And let's face it, I am looking to sell this book. So I am going to skip my good dating stories that I know and go right into marriages.

You found her (or him) the one and only person you want to spend the rest of your life with. The man proposed the woman accepted. You are both so happy you can't wait for the big day to come. (More so for the woman than the man...lol!!) For many couples the wedding is the beginning of the end for them. See a lot of people out there think that the wedding is the most important thing and let me tell you this. A WEDDING DOES NOT MAKE A MARRIAGE. You get that? I will repeat it; A wedding does not make a marriage. The wedding is not the most important thing in the world. I agree it should be nice, it should be important, but it should not be the most important thing.

That statement reminds me of a movie called *IT TAKES TWO* starring George Newbern and Leslie Hope as 2 kids that have known each other their whole lives and are going to get married. In this movie the guy is looking to buy a new car for him and his bride. He has to travel from his little town to the big city to buy this. He is continually trying to talk to his fiancé about everything including the car but she is so caught up in making the wedding perfect she forgets about him. She just tells him to do whatever he wants to do basically. He goes to buy this car, but winds up having problems with it and the dealership screwed him over by putting in inferior parts in it because he didn't buy the warranty. So, because he didn't buy the warranty nothing is covered, and the dealer is trying to get him to pay for everything as an extra charge. He tries calling his fiancé and talking to her but she keeps brushing him off because all she cares about is the wedding. He winds up hooking up with his hot sales lady and wondering if he truly wants to be married at all now. He feels like he is being put to the side for the wedding. He winds up missing the rehearsal dinner and when he finally calls her she rips into him instead of listening yet again. So he calls his dad who talked him down from the proverbial ledge and he decides to come home. But first he trashes the car dealership and his hot saleslady makes it where he has a receipt showing his car paid in full. He was running late for the wedding and his bride stood up in front of everyone and told them that she was so caught up in the wedding that she ignored him and that it was all her fault don't blame him and that apparently being married is not what he wanted or needed. Right then he walks in and says that is exactly what he needed. They wind up getting married and lived happily ever after. Great story right? Not really. Unfortunately that is happening way too much in real life. People get so caught up in the wedding that they forget they have their whole life to spend with this person. I experienced this exact scenario with my second wife.

My story goes like this. I dated her for about 2 months before I determined she was the one I wanted to be with. We talked about our future we talked about everything people should talk about. I finally proposed to her after we had been together for 5 months on a trip I had won to Cancun Mexico. Oh wait, you have to hear the proposal story. First off my ex-wife (girlfriend at the time) had been living with her parents at the time I found out I won this trip. And her parents said in no way shape or form is she going to be living under their roof and going to Mexico with me. So she moved into an apartment on her own not far from where I lived. (Yeah right moved in.) She never spent one night there. She put her furniture there and wound up subletting it to a woman she worked with. The whole time she supposedly lived there she actually lived with me and my 2 kids. So now that she didn't live with them she figured it was OK for her to go with me to Cancun now. So back to the proposal story. I went to a guy that I sold a car to that made jewelry and told him how much I had and what I wanted. He made a very nice custom ring with the little bit of money I had. And it looked perfect, let me tell you. I put that ring in my carry on bag for our trip. I wanted this proposal to be very special. I wanted everything to be perfect. We got to the airport and my carry on was too big. They wanted me to check it. I fought it. She kept saying what is the big deal just check it in. I finally did check the bag. I hate checking bags because I don't want them lost. Especially this one with its precious cargo. (That reminds me of one of my favorite jokes..."I went to the airport and told the lady taking my bags that I wanted the first one sent to California and the second one sent to New York. She told me that is not possible. I said sure it is! You guys did it last time and I didn't even have to ask you to...dang I crack myself up) Anywho we get on the plane and sure enough it is delayed for some problem. As we sat there for almost an hour I grabbed my cell phone and called the airline. I told them what flight I was on and they said that particular flight was being canceled so I said to put me on the next flight and they did. I am sure glad I called because of all the people on that flight I was the only one that got on the other flight because I made that phone call. I proceeded to ask "what about my checked luggage will that be transferred to the new plane?" The airline assured me it would be, but I was still very worried. I mean come on I just checked this engagement ring against my better wishes and now this. It was a very long flight to Miami (Miami because we had to change planes there). We finally get to Miami and I am asking everyone I can about my bags if they are on my new flight and being transferred to my new plane. As I keep asking she is constantly telling me to quit worrying about it, if they get lost we can replace the clothes in Mexico. Yeah right. Like that was my only concern, my clothes.

We finally arrive in Mexico and I am now sweating bullets because my bag is not on the luggage carousel. Round and round it goes and nothing. Then finally no bags are left. What the hell? I start looking for anyone that can help me. Then I saw it. It was sitting off to the side of the carousel hidden from me because someone removed it thinking it was theirs, but when they realized it wasn't they didn't put it back on the carousel. Of course by that time I was a nervous wreck. She kept asking me why I got so freaked out with all of this. "It happens" she kept saying over and over again.

We finally get to the resort where we were staying. All be it 4 hours later than the other contest winners. We go up to our room and the bellhop was showing us the room and the safe. The safe...ahh perfect! I can put the ring there until I am ready to make it perfect. Then I thought...hell no. The way my day is going that bellhop would come back after we left and steal it. Or I would lose the key to the safe. So I put the ring in my pocket and changed my whole proposal plan. I was not going to go through with my original plan of proposing under water while scuba diving. I thought she would freak and spit out her breather and die and that would be a bad engagement story wouldn't it? The other reason is I wasn't going to do it underwater is I was afraid something would happen between the first night we were there and our scuba trip which was on the third day of the trip. So I decided that the first night would be it.

We went to the welcome dinner that was planned for all the contest winners. I was telling everyone what I was planning to do every chance I had when she went to the washroom, or to grab a drink, or whatever she did when she walked away. Everybody was so excited and they actually did a good job of keeping it quiet when she came back. Dinner was finally over and we start walking hand in hand on the beach. I decide it is go time. I drop to one knee with the ring in its box in my hand. The ocean at my back the stars shining bright in the Mexican sky and I finally ask her to marry me. Before she could say yes I get knocked over by a huge wave. I land in her arms and she says yes. (Maybe that wave was God trying to tell me something? Like don't do it dummy!!) Pretty cool story huh?

Back to my "the wedding doesn't make a marriage story". We decided we were going to get married in August the following year. I had to get my first marriage annulled to get married in the Catholic Church and her dad wouldn't allow her to get married anywhere else because and I quote "The Catholic Church takes the sacrament of marriage very seriously and once you are married in the Catholic Church it means forever." (What a crock that turned out to be and I will explain that later in the Organized Religion is messed up chapter.) The annulment was going to take at least six months, so we had to move the wedding date to November as opposed to the original August date that we originally wanted. So now that it was going to be 6 months before we got married she had plenty of time to plan my funeral...I mean plan our wedding. And plan she did.

We decided to have the wedding reception at a resort in between our 2 families. Almost exactly in the middle. That was the only place we both could agree on. That however was the last decision I had to make or be involved in. I was not allowed to make any more decisions. I was not consulted on any more things after that. She and her family took over from there. She told me what color to get for the tuxedos, how many guys I would need based on the wedding party that she wanted. Just an FYI on that, I had to find 11 guys to stand up, 9 groomsmen and 2 ushers, can you say overkill. I had the guys no problem I just thought it was excessive. She told me her brother's gift to us was going to be the DJ. I told her that was cool and when do I get to help pick the music. Man oh man you should have seen the look I got then. Needless to say I didn't help pick out any of the music. And the music was terrible. If I wanted to hear beeping and buzzing as dance music I would have brought my alarm clock and saved the DJ fee. I did however, get to go to the food tasting for the reception. I liked some of the food and the cake. The stuff that I liked she and her mom didn't like, so yep you guessed it they won again. Then it came time for the invitations and the seating chart. 300 people will be in attendance. Of which 45 people were my side of the family and my friends. Originally I had about 100 people on my list but there were members of her family coming from other states just to come to this wedding and we had to make room. I had to cut people from my list because there wasn't enough room. Yeah not enough room for my friends and family but there was plenty of room for people she hadn't seen in years or even met before. You know, friends of her parents, friends of her aunts and uncles, people we didn't know or would ever see again. This is how selfish she was and still is. I am a pretty good guy and I wanted her to be happy with everything, so I didn't really care as long as she was happy I figured I was going to be happy too. (Unfortunately, I should have seen this as a precursor to how our married life would be.) After all was said and done the wedding and the reception cost her father (thank God I didn't pay for it) almost 40,000 dollars. Yep you read it right 40,000 dollars. Everything had to be perfect and it was for her, but not for me, and certainly not for us as a couple. I felt like an outsider at my own wedding. She was so caught up in making everything right she didn't realize the one thing that was most important. This was supposed to be a celebration of our love. Instead it was a huge family reunion that I happened to be invited to.

This is what I am talking about. It didn't matter how much money was spent on the wedding and reception. It didn't matter where the wedding and reception was held. It didn't matter how big the wedding party was or how many people were in attendance. All that matters is 2 people that love each other share their vows with God, themselves, and some close family as witnesses. If you are truly in love with your partner that means that it doesn't matter where it is, when it is, or who is there, as long as you are together.

There was my perfect example of how a wedding does not make a marriage. But a wedding can put some unnecessary stress on your marriage if you do not listen to your partner. Ask him or her for an opinion and when they give it to you listen to it and work together to find a way to where you are both happy with the decision. It is not about the wedding, the reception or even the honeymoon. It is about starting a life together. And that is the key word...TOGETHER!!

Marriage is about working together for each other. It is about compromise, give and take, and about loving one another for the rest of your life. It is not about who has the upper hand in the marriage. It is not about pleasing other people outside of your house. Marriage is the joining of 2 people as 1 body and 1 soul. It is you and your spouse against the world together. Your first priority is your new spouse and family. My wife obviously did not pay attention in the pre-wedding classes we took for 4 weeks.

It was my wedding day that I started to see the true woman I was in love with. And although my wife was pretty on the outside she was not on the inside. She was far from it. All she cared about from then on was pleasing herself and her family. We were married less than one month before she decided that she didn't like her engagement ring anymore and it didn't go with her wedding band well enough. So I went to a jeweler by where I worked (the original guy went out of business... go figure.) and let her decide what she wanted. He used the center stone from the original ring for her new ring and designed it to match the wedding band. Both of her rings now had diamonds covering the whole band and they lined up with each other. It took him over a week to make it. We went and picked it up and she was happy with her new ring or at least seemed to be happy. (See a selfish pattern here at all?) The original ring was pretty much destroyed because he had to remove the center stone and it was in there pretty good. I guess my original guy was good but not good enough to stay in business. My wife still wanted to keep the ring anyway. Later that night she suddenly burst into tears because she wanted the original ring back. She didn't like the new one as much as she thought she would. I kept telling her that it will be fine and she will learn to love it and it didn't matter what ring she had as long as we were together. But all she kept saying is that she was sorry she ever changed it and kept right on crying.

Her family had a problem with the cars I owned. Saying they were not practical. I owned a 1996 Corvette and a 2000 Sebring convertible. She drove the convertible as a family car and my corvette was my get back and forth to work car and it was used for whenever we just went out as a couple. A year into our marriage I had to get rid of the Corvette because I was sick of hearing how impractical it was to have. It seemed like everyday I heard from her or her family about this. Actually I didn't hear about it from her family I had to hear her complain about how her family was riding her about the car. So needless to say I traded it in for a 2003 Durango. This was now her car and I took the convertible. My payment went up 200 dollars to get a car I didn't want, but hey, it made her happy so I did it. See, I can compromise. I can give when it needs to be done. All she could do was take and take and take.

After we were married we talked about her staying home with my 2 kids (Tim and Ashlee) from my first marriage, so when they got home from school one of us would always be there. So she went from full time at her job to part time. She would work only until 1 pm so when the kids got out of school she could either pick them up or at the very least be home when they got there. I was making enough money to support us like that so it was great. Coming home to my happy family.

It was at this time we decided to have a baby together. You see, early on we decided it was going to be 5 years into our marriage before we were going to try and have a baby. But after a year and a half we thought it would be the right time. My wife went off the pill and that first month of trying we had success. She was pregnant. We planned it perfectly too. The baby was going to be born after the Superbowl and before baseball season started. This way we didn't have to miss any good sports...lol!!

We were all very excited to have this baby. That is until my wife found out it was going to be a baby girl. She wanted a boy. She cried for what seemed like weeks but it was only days. All I kept telling her was to just pray for a healthy baby girl. That is all I ever cared about when it came to my kids. I just wanted a healthy baby. 10 fingers and 10 toes, you know what I mean? Well my wife blamed me for that. She kept saying over and over again to me that it is the mans sperm that determines the sex of the baby and that I must not have it in me. I did once seeing how I have a son. Yes I have one son and three girls. And let me tell you it makes for interesting times around my house.

It was about then that things started going down hill. She decided that with her having the baby she wanted to stay home all day and I agreed because statistics show that a child that has 2 parents, and the mom stays home to take care of the children, the children do better in life. At the same time this happened, business at the dealership I was at started to slow down. It was getting worse and worse. I am a 100% commission guy so if business goes south so does my pay. It was getting harder and harder to make ends meet.

Then it came time for my baby to be born. We actually had a regular doctors appointment planned for that day and when we were driving there my wife started complaining about pains in her lower back. I told her she is going into labor and she said no she isn't and I didn't know what I was talking about. So we saw the doctor and guess what? Yep, you guessed it. I was right!! My wife was indeed going into labor. We started driving to the hospital seeing how the contractions were like 15 minutes apart. We were calling everyone to tell them where we were headed . By the time we got to the hospital half her family was already there. (I am being sarcastic, but I am the writer of this after all, in actuality only her mom and dad were there.) Her brother was on his way from Chicago. Her sister was on her way home from college. And my wife wouldn't want to give birth without her sister being in the room with us. I stayed with my wife the whole time encouraging her, holding her hand, and getting her anything she needed. That was until her sister arrived. Then it was all about her sister helping her and being there for her. I was on the outside yet again.

During the labor I got up and went to the washroom. I came out and doctors and nurses were scrambling around the delivery room because the baby's heart rate dropped drastically and they were trying to figure out what was going on. What a coincidence, so was I. I had no idea and I didn't want to ask because I didn't want to bother the medical staff with my worry. I just watched my wife and held her hand. They finally stabilized the baby's heartbeat and then it was time for little baby Sara to come out. It was a great day and I actually cried because I was so happy. I went out into the waiting area to tell everyone that was there that Sara was healthy, but low and behold while I was in there comforting my wife and crying tears of joy at the same time, her sister beat me to it. That woman stole my thunder as a new dad. When I did reach the waiting room everyone was already congratulating me, and my wife's sister then proceeded to tell everyone there that I was crying, and then said to her mom, dad, and brother, and I quote "what a pussy!" Can you believe that? I was worried about my baby girl and my wife when the heart rate dropped and I was happy that they both came out healthy and cried tears of happiness and all my sister-in-law could do was call me names. I guess it says a lot for what kind of selfish person she was.

It was weird, only the kids in that family were selfish. My wife's parents were probably the most caring and giving people I ever met. They were always there for their kids and other peoples kids too. They took my kids into that family without even missing a beat and with out thinking twice about it. They were so generous that when I was struggling to support us all they helped pay for the house until business was able to pick up for me. The kids were so spoiled that if things were not given to them easily they didn't want them. And if things didn't go their way they would get upset and pout until they got their way. I was raised very poor and had to earn everything I have ever had. Where as these kids had things handed to them on a silver platter. I remember a few times that I could not afford something my wife wanted and she said it was OK because all she had to do was ask her daddy and he would get it for her, and he always did. I actually feel bad for my ex in-laws. These people are nice but oblivious to what is going on in their own family. Their son is gay and told everyone in the family and swore them to secrecy because he didn't tell his parents because he thinks his dad would cut him off financially. But those stories are for another book. (Yep, I am pretty sure I can write a whole other book on just that family alone.)

Fast forward to October 31, 2005. My baby Sara is a year and a half old and we are at my brother and sister in law's house. We had a nice family tradition of going to all the families houses for trick or treating and then going out trick or treating with all my wife's cousins after we visited the families. So we are sitting there talking about how we want to have another baby soon and if it is a boy we were going to name it Matthew George. We both liked the name Matthew for a boy and George was my grandfather's first name and it was also my wife's father's name. So it was a perfect name for our son because I had a lot of respect for both George's. And it was great tribute to them.

And then it happened. It wasn't like rain on a parade, it was more like a nuclear bomb being dropped right on my forehead. It was almost 2 weeks to the day that my wife told me she didn't want to be married anymore. Her exact words were "I don't want to be married anymore. Not just to you but to anybody. This is not how I pictured married life to be. I want to move back home with my mom and dad. I had more fun there." How can you say that just 2 weeks after talking about having another baby? I started to wonder all kinds of things. Was she having an affair? Was her witch of a sister behind this? You know the typical things.

I told her we shouldn't give up so easily and we should go through counseling first and keep trying. Marriage is a commitment for life and we swore before God in a catholic church that we would be together forever. She said she didn't want to go to counseling and she didn't have to go if she didn't want to. I went without her to visit the priest of the church we were married in, and he said there was nothing he could do. He said "if a man wants to leave his wife, and she wants to work it out, she usually can get him to at least listen and go to counseling. But when a woman makes up her mind to leave there is usually nothing you can do to stop it." I even made an appointment for her to visit the priest based on the premise of her just talking to him about me and how to help me because I was battling depression at this point. Of course I was battling depression, my job was not doing well at this point, the woman I wanted to spend my life with wants to leave, and she is taking my daughter with her. I don't know a person in this world that would not be depressed at this point. If there is such a person, I sure as heck don't want to meet him or her because they have no soul. She moved out after the new year because she didn't want to upset the kids before Christmas and ruin the holiday's for them. Well, I have news for all that are reading this, kids can sense problems in a parent's relationship.

I finally convinced her to go to counseling because I told her if she didn't go through counseling I would fight the divorce and drag it out for as long as I possibly could. Well, there was a waste of 200 dollars for that counseling session. She came to the counseling and sat there the whole time saying how she did nothing wrong. How it is all my fault and that I need to change completely but not for her because she is never coming back. (Oh I forgot to tell you that I found out she was indeed having an affair with a married man. A man that was the father of a boy that played on my son's football team. She denies it to this day but I found all kinds of text messages on her phone from him and one night she went out with a friend that came to visit her from Wisconsin and while they were out they called this guy about a half dozen times early in the evening and then at 2 am after they got home.) She continued to say how she was a great person and how I was lucky she stayed as long as she did, you know the usual "I am better than everyone" thing that she had about her. It was 2 hours of this. I barely got a word in edgewise. The last things this counselor said to my wife was "you realize that this whole time you blamed Todd for everything but it is you who is breaking your vows. It is you not trying to make things work. You yourself told me right here that you told him that you were leaving because of all these things but you didn't tell him that you were upset about it and when you did you had already made up your mind to leave. How is that fair to him? So once again I say you are not living up to being a wife and you should give your marriage a chance because you haven't done that yet." My wife replied "I don't want to and I don't have to do anything I don't want to do."

During our divorce my wife didn't let my daughter spend the night (and she still doesn't because my wife used my depression against me and told the courts that I would not be able to take care of her.) and I only get to see her on my days off. She wanted the divorce her way. No negotiating with her. She used every dirty trick in the book to make sure I couldn't fight for what I deserve and what my daughter deserves.

What she doesn't understand, and most divorcing couple's don't understand either, is what effects divorce has on the kids. People like my ex-wife are so caught up in what they think is best for themselves that they only think of themselves and not the kids. I truly do not think it is right to stay in a relationship just because of the kids. I do however think you should exhaust all efforts to salvage the relationship before resorting to a divorce. That means you go to counseling. You try and understand one another all over again. You actually work at it and not just quit.

There was a reason you married your spouse. For our children's sake, for our economy's sake, and for our country's sake this should be happening. Yes I said our economy and country. Divorces bring down our economy by diminishing the family and hurting people's credit do to the cost. Our overall country lies within the American family. There have been many studies showing that kids that come from a divorced household are more likely to drop out of school, commit a crime, be divorced themselves, create teen pregnancies, and thus repeat this vicious circle. These trends need to stop, and they need to stop now.

You may be asking yourselves how does divorce affect the economy? That is why I am here writing this book. So I can explain how our economy is affected by divorce and how our decisions affect this whole country for that matter.

Since marriage is a legal civil contract, the only way to dissolve it is through court proceedings which means that all divorces, both amicable and messy, require some court time and resources which adds to the already heavy load of work clogging our court system. While some of the costs of the court system are offset by fees paid by participants coming before the courts, taxpayers still have to pay a large part of the bill for the court system. Let us not forget that when the court system is forced to increase in size due to increasing business the taxpayers have to pay for that as well.

Litigants in other areas, besides marriage, are also burdened by the increased divorce proceedings as the additional load on the courts causes longer wait times for everyone. Since in business "time is money", especially in this day and age, these delays add to the costs of business litigation which, in turn, is passed on to consumers.

There are also costs to the social service system, since the after divorce income and living expenses are not always equal usually leaving one, or occasionally both, spouses below the official poverty line which makes them eligible for things like food stamps, government paid housing, government paid medical care and even possible cash welfare payments. The cost of these programs are all paid for by us the taxpayers. And let's not forget the cost of running these programs. The more people that go on these programs after a divorce the more people that need to be hired to administrate them. Mo' money, Mo' money, Mo money.

I have mentioned that a divorce affects the kids. There have been many studies to prove what I am talking about. One of these studies was conducted by the University of Missouri in 2008 and posted on classbrain.com. The study was titled ***FOCUS ON THE KIDS: THE EFFECTS OF DIVORCE ON CHILDREN.*** Here are some relevant things that I picked up from this article that most people that are going to seek a divorce didn't realize their kids will experience.

This is how an infant will think and react to the divorce according to this study:

What the child understands

Does not understand conflict, but may react to changes in parents' energy level and mood.

Possible child reactions

Loss of appetite.

Upset stomach — may spit up more. More fretful or anxious.

Here is how a toddler will think and react the divorce according to this study:

What the child understands

Understands that a parent has moved away, but doesn't understand why.

Possible child reactions

More crying, clinging.

Problems sleeping.

Regression to infant behaviors.

May feel anger, may not understand why he/she feels that way.

May worry when parent is out of sight.

May withdraw, bite or be irritable.

Here is what a preschooler will think and react to the divorce according to this study:

What the child understands

Doesn't understand what separation or divorce means. Realizes one parent is not as active in their lives.

Possible child reactions

Pleasant and unpleasant fantasies.

Feels uncertain about the future.

May feel responsible.

May hold anger inside.

Feels that he/she should be punished.

May be accident prone.

May become aggressive and angry toward parent he/she lives with.

May have more nightmares.

Experiences feelings of grief because of sudden absence of parent.

Here is how a child in early elementary school will think and react to the divorce according to this study:

What the child understands

Begins to understand what a divorce is and understands that her/his parents won't live together anymore and that they don't love each other.

Possible child reactions

Feels deceived and feels a sense of loss.

Hopes parents will get back together.

Feels rejected by the parent who left.

Ignores school and friendships.

Worries about the future.

Fears nobody will be there to pick him/her up from school.

Complains of headaches or stomachaches.

Has trouble sleeping.

Tries to recreate "what was."

Experiences loss of appetite, sleep problems, diarrhea, urinary frequency.

And last but not least this is how an adolescent and preteen will think and react to the divorce based on this study:

What the child understands

Understands but doesn't accept the divorce.

Possible child reactions

Feels angry and disillusioned.

Feels abandoned, that parent is leaving him/her not the other spouse.

Tries to take advantage of parents' low energy and high stress levels.

Tries to take control over family.

Shows extreme behavior (good and bad).

Becomes moralistic, or becomes involved in high-risk behaviors (drugs, shoplifting, skipping school).

Tries to be an "angel," to bring the family back together.

Tries to cut one or both parents out of her/his life.

Feels as if he/she will never be able to have a long-term relationship.

Feels like he/she must grow up too soon.

Worries about financial matters.

This next study I found really says exactly what I am trying to point out. It is interesting enough to quote verbatim in this book so I am going to post the whole study here.

Children reared in fatherless homes are more than twice as likely to become male adolescent delinquents or teen mothers, according to a significant new study by two economists at the University of California, Santa Barbara.

Llad Phillips and William S. Comanor based their research on data from random surveys of 15,000 youths conducted annually by the Center for Human Resources at Ohio State University. Their findings suggest that current proposals to provide tax credits and exemptions for single mothers and to collect more child support from absent fathers will have little effect on the problem of delinquency among teenage boys.

"Both measures tacitly accept the father's absence from the home and seek to ameliorate its consequences by increasing the income available to mother and child. However, it requires an increase in family income of approximately $50,000 to counter the father's absence," the economists wrote in a report outlining the results of their study, which were presented at the Western Economics Association meeting in San Francisco on July 1.

Phillips and Comanor designed their study to account for the influence of income, and found that in the case of boys, a minimum of $54,000 in additional family income is necessary to counter the harmful effects of absent fathers. For girls, the figure is much lower-$17,000 a year. The researchers also found that while absent mothers have a negligible impact on male adolescent delinquency, motherless homes are 56 percent more likely to result in teen pregnancy among girls.

"The absence of either parent has a significant effect on the kids having one kind of pathology or another, but the absence of a father tends to have a more significant effect, and it seems to more seriously affect the sons," said Phillips,

whose research also indicates that step-fathers may in fact contribute to the problem.

"The effect of the presence or absence of moms and dads on childbearing at a young age among girls are more equal than their effect on delinquency by boys."

"A lot of kids get involved in crime long before they are able to make rational choices about crime vs. legitimate work," Phillips says. "And that's our motivation in doing this research-finding out the importance of the family in the whole process."

Now as a parent I know I do not want to put my kids through all of this without trying every possible option there is first. I truly do not think I am in the minority here. I have faith in people and believe that all parents want what is best for kids but do not realize what the kids are going to be put through because, like my ex wife, all they care about is themselves.

Another thing I took from this study that shocked me is the fact that our government is trying to pass legislation that will give tax breaks and exemptions to single mothers. How bout giving tax breaks to married couples that have children and stay married? Why not try and save the sanctity of marriage? Why not save the American family?

Divorces in this country are too easy to get. A friend of mine just told me that her friend got divorced for 250 dollars over the INTERNET All her friend had to do was show up the day that court was set. Are you kidding me? Is this what this country is coming to? Eventually it will happen that when you get married you get a predetermined divorce agreement and when the time comes for you to get divorced you both sign it and send it in to the proper county clerk. Bing, bang, boom, you are divorced. No court date, no bickering, no problem, right? Wrong!! Big problem. We should be making divorces harder to get, not easier. Why is everyone so set on ending the American family?

There are no rules in place to prevent divorces from happening. Sure there are rules when it comes to the kids, for instance you have to go to a divorced parenting class that shows you how to act around your kids. Where are the classes for people that are to help you in your marriage no matter what? Where are the classes to keep marriages together? I have said before there is a reason that you married your spouse. Why not try and find that magic again?

In Illinois there is a 2 year "cooling off period" requirement before your divorce can be final. According to dictionary.com the meaning of the word requirement is: that which is required; a thing demanded or obligatory, a need or necessity. Now here is the kicker, you can wave the 2 years if you choose to. So is that really a requirement? I say it is an option not a requirement.

I am going to fix the divorce problem in this country right now. Come on, you knew I had a fix for it, didn't you? I am going to give a true list of requirements that will stop the divorces from being so easy. We need a 1 year required (truly required can't wave it. With the exception of life threatening violence situations.) couples counseling for all people wishing to be divorced. This counseling would be paid for by the individuals involved in the divorce, it must be done by a licensed marriage counselor in the respective community that the married couple lives in. The counselor will have an obligation to keep notes and report to the court the progress of the couple. The counseling would be at minimum 2 times per month. That means 24 minimum marriage counseling sessions would be required.

Will this required counseling stop all divorces from happening? Absolutely not. It will however make people think before trying to get divorced. It will also make people think before they get married on a whim. I know I sure would have thought differently before getting married if I knew that it would be required of me to go through 1 year of counseling at my expense. Not that I planned on being divorced but I sure would have gone a lot slower and gotten to know my wife better before hand. And I am sure a lot of people in this country would do the same.

And now probably the most controversial chapter of this book...

ORGANIZED RELIGION

This particular chapter I saved for last because I am sure it will be the most controversial chapter in this whole book. There are more situations that rise out of religion in this world than anything else. My God is better than your God, my God told me to kill you because you don't believe in him and you believe in another God, my God blah, blah, blah, blah!!! I am just sick of hearing all of this nonsense. I do believe in God and I do believe that Jesus Christ died for my sins. (If you do not believe what I believe, I do not have a problem with that, I will not force my beliefs on you and I request you do not force your beliefs on me.) I am not referring to God or any God for that matter in this chapter however. I am referring to churches, synagogues, mosques, temples,and any organized religion in this country. I am doing this because I see what is happening in our religious organizations throughout this country. Oh, and let us not forget how religion affects our government.

I will first tackle how religion is in our government. This country was founded by people fleeing religious persecution. Our constitution actually states freedom of religion. I am cool with that. What I am not cool with is the fact that they say that we have freedom of religion but whenever Christmas comes up it is not allowed to be Christmas anymore because you can not offend non Christians. Now we have "Happy Holidays" instead of "Merry Christmas". Yet all of our businesses are closed on Christmas day and not Happy Holiday day? We let our kids have Christmas break but we are not allowed to have Christmas pageants at school. If a Christian puts up something about Christmas and it offends a Muslim person the Christian is suddenly wrong and has to remove it. But if Muslims put up anything about their religion and a Christian says something about it the Christian is now accused of religious hating?

We all know about the separation of church and state. Well here is proof that it truly does not exist. Right now our government is in one of the hottest debates and it involves the church. The debate is over the right for gay people to marry. What is the main reason that our government doesn't want gays to marry? They say it is because it is against God. Whoa!! Wait one minute. How can something that is against God be illegal if church and state are separate? I personally think that gay people should have the right to marry. I want them to have to suffer like the rest of us that have been, will be, or currently are married. I think it is only fair, don't you?

All I am saying is you can't have it both ways government. Either stay out of religion or not, but make up your mind and don't pick and choose what you are not involved in.

That is enough about government and religion, now on to the real problem with organized religion. It doesn't matter what religion you are, what I am about to say is true for all organized religions. (I will get into one specific religion later but I am going to lump them all together for now). I have been to many churches and even visited a synagogue once, and they all do the same thing. They ask for money. They continually ask for money. The Christians believe you should give 10% of your gross earnings to the church. Why? Do you really think that god is going to be ticked at me if I don't? Will I not be allowed into heaven if I do not give the church my money? What is this money used for? I know we are all told that it goes for the betterment of the church and all the charity work they do. But truly where does this money go? I am sure some of it goes to the church and some of it goes to the work they do. I am not saying the church doesn't do good things for people. But everything I have seen the church do charity wise involves donations of whatever is needed. They give food to people who need it, but that food comes from food drives. They give clothes to people that need them, but again, the clothes comes from clothing drives. And the people running these drives donate their time so they are not getting paid out of the money that people give every week. This is yet another example of one nation under the dollar that I spoke about earlier. And this is only one of the reasons I do not like organized religion.

I think the biggest crooked organization in this world (outside of our government that is) is the Catholic Church. This church alone influences governments of many countries. It is the largest political power in this country. The Catholic Church has over 860 million members in the world. Almost one fifth of the entire human population is Catholic.

I personally got to experience the greed and corruptness of the Catholic Church first hand. My ex wife was a Catholic as I had stated earlier, and I went to church with her, I even had my two oldest kids baptized in the Catholic Church. I admit I was brainwashed into believing that the Catholic Church was indeed the best church to be a member of. Boy was I wrong! Not only was I wrong, but it was proven to me over and over again by the church itself.

This greed is proven every Sunday at a Catholic Church. They take your tithing, as they call it, and then they ask for a second tithing for something special that the church is going to do for the community. "This week we are going to take a second collection for our missionaries in Guatemala (or where ever they are talking about this week). OK, here is my question; what is the first tithing for? Is it for bail money for priests? Is it for the electric bill? No, really what is it for? I actually watched people give and give and give to this church every week and if it wasn't money that they were giving it was their time that they gave to the church for volunteer work to help the church get bigger and stronger. Why? How big of a church is needed? How much money does it cost to run the church? All churches are income tax free and when they buy any property they don't have to pay any sales tax either. So they take money in from hard working people and do what with it? In my opinion it is just another version of a Ponzi scheme without the payout on your investment. The top of the Ponzi scheme in this case is The Vatican. They are worse than the government in this case. At least with the government you get the illusion that your money is being used wisely for programs (and sometimes it actually is being used wisely, but most of the time it isn't). In the Catholic Church they just take your money, and take some more, and even take some more, with nothing given to you for it. My friend here just told me that he was Catholic and associated them with an insurance company. I disagreed with him saying that with an insurance company at least they will be there for you if you need them. It is piece of mind. The Catholic Church takes your money and they tell you lie after lie after lie.

Why must these collections be taken? At my Catholic wedding a collection plate was taken around. Why? At a Catholic funeral a collection plate is passed around. Again, why? In Acts 8:20 it says the gift of God is not to be purchased with money. So are the Catholics going against the word of God here? I believe they are. They are trying to have you purchase God by giving all you can until you just can't give any more. I would truly love to see the church's budget, how it is all spent, and exactly how much money was collected. Every time I think about the church and the money they collect, I think of a Simpsons episode where Reverend Lovejoy was in the back room putting the change in a change counter and he was singing and whistling. In yet another Simpsons episode Ned Flanders was going up to the reverend for advice and he put the collection plate in front of him and cleared his throat and looked away insinuating that he wanted money first. When Ned finally did put some change in the plate the reverend helped him. So Ned couldn't get any guidance without first paying for it. This is how I see all organized religions right now (especially the Catholic Church), money hungry entities bent on their own agenda.

How come more things are not being done for the betterment of our communities by our churches? Where is all this money going? Why are they not spending money to help people in need in our communities? I'll tell you why!! The money that is collected by the church goes to pay off all of the lawsuits they are involved in because of the molestation charges . How else can you explain the Catholic Church coming up with millions upon millions of dollars to pay these people off?

Now that I brought it up let us talk about the legal aspects of what is going on in the Catholic church. Priests molesting children is at the forefront. I was actually just reading some of the stories about priests and the children that they molested. I can not list them all here but there were over 10,000 incidents that have been reported with more coming. This alone could be another whole book. I could title it "come on feel the boys" or "church where the priests make Michael Jackson look like Jesus." Too much? Maybe it would be, but you get my drift. There are stories of cover ups and actual gag orders on people that have been abused. This is so these people will not speak out about the abuse that had to endure.

Why do you suppose these people are being forced to not talk? Oh, and do not forget about the people that received cash settlements for the abuse. These people also signed gag orders or they would not receive their money from the Catholic Church. The Catholic Church wants to keep it quiet so they can keep the stranglehold on the people that still believe the Catholic Church is a good thing. We need to stop believing in the Catholic Church. I think God is important but the Church is just looking out for itself, not the people, and certainly not God.

Here is an example of what money can get you in the Catholic Church. An annulment. If you have enough money to donate to the church you can get whatever you want from them including the right to break a holy sacrament. Keep reading and you will see what I am talking about and I am talking from my own personal experience on this one.

Among the Catholic community, one of the most sensitive and most avoided topics is divorce and its consequences. The Catholic Church teaches the Gospel of Matthew:

"And Pharisees came up to him and tested him by asking, 'Is it lawful to divorce one's wife for any cause?' He answered, 'Have you not read that he who made them from the beginning made them male and female, and said, "For this reason a man shall leave his father and mother and be joined to his wife, and the two shall become one"? So they are no longer two but one. What therefore God has joined together, let not man put asunder.' They said to him, 'Why then did Moses command one to give a certificate of divorce, and to put her away?' He said to them, 'For your hardness of heart Moses allowed you to divorce your wives, but from the beginning it was not so. And I say to you: whoever divorces his wife, except for unchastity, and marries another, commits adultery; and he who marries a divorced woman, commits adultery.'"

This is how the Catholic Church defines divorce:

"Divorce is a grave offense against the natural law. It claims to break the contract, to which the spouses freely consented, to live with each other until death. Sacramental marriage is the sign of the covenant of salvation, to which divorce does incredible injury. Contracting a new union, even if it is recognized by civil law, adds to the gravity of the rupture: the remarried spouse is then in a situation of public and permanent adultery. If a husband, separated from his wife, becomes involved with another woman, he is an adulterer because he makes that woman commit adultery; and the woman who lives with him is an adulteress, because she has drawn another's husband to herself.

Furthermore, the Catechism states that divorce is immoral because "it introduces disorder into the family and into society. This disorder brings grave harm to the deserted spouse, to children traumatized by the separation of their parents and often torn between them, and because of its contagious effect which makes it truly a plague on society."

Let me get this straight. God and Jesus himself say that divorce is wrong. The Catechism states that divorce is immoral. Everything in the Catholic Church says that divorce is immoral. Why is it that Catholic people still get divorced and the church allows them to get remarried in the Catholic Church after an annulment? This is possible because all you have to do is give them money to allow you to whatever you want.

An annulment is obtained by one of the parties involved in the divorce going to the diocese and requesting it in writing. According to the rules of the annulment, the circumstances of the failed marriage are to be thoroughly reviewed by two groups of church experts in two different diocese and it is to be determined by both groups that the marriage bond was never truly formed. What determines this bond? Is it consummation (sex)? Is it the ceremony performed in the Catholic Church before God and witnesses? Or is it the birth of a child to this couple? I think these are interesting questions. The Catholic Church actually doesn't care about any of this. As I stated earlier all they care about is the money. Want more proof? Good because I have another part to this story.

After my girlfriend and I had gotten engaged and determined when and where we were going to get married we had to go to the church to set up the pre-marriage class that the church requires you to go through or you can not get married in the Church. There were 2 options for this class. One class that was for half a Saturday or 4 weeks at a church qualified persons home for one hour each week. Because I work in the car business and Saturday is our busiest day, we decided the 4 weeks at the persons home would be the best way to go. The people that were chosen by the diocese lived relatively close to where we lived and it actually was a good group of people. There were a total of 6 couples in this class. In this class we had to learn how to do things the Catholic Church way when it came to marriage. We were not allowed to use birth control (which we did), we were not allowed to be cohabitating with each other before the wedding(which we were doing), no premarital sex (which there was), and many other things that we were taught so we were allowed to be married in the Catholic Church. (I forgot to tell you that this class wasn't free either. I do not remember the exact amount but I know it was more than 100 bucks.)

We did go through this class, we "graduated", and got a little certificate to prove we did. We were now allowed to get married in the Catholic Church with God's blessing. We were married a few months later knowing how to do everything the Catholic way.

Now here is where the problem comes in. We had to go through all of this to get married in the Catholic Church, but when it came time for my wife to decide that she didn't want to be married anymore, there was nothing the church could do. There is no class that the church requires to get divorced. There is no required counseling. There is nothing in place to keep a marriage together.

I have been divorced now for going on 3 years. We have been apart for almost 4 years and my ex wife actually gave me a piece of paper a few months ago requesting a release of my personal information from my personal therapist. (I was seeing a therapist after we split up because like I told you before I was battling depression.) This request was actually from the diocese that her church was a part of. Needless to say I threw this request out. I am not going to share my personal therapy sessions with anyone, let alone the church. I later received a questionnaire from the same diocese asking my version of the divorce and I got to see what my wife was telling them as to why we were divorced. Her whole story was made up. This is a woman that swears by the Catholic Church but is lying to them so she can get what she wants.

Instead of answering the questionnaire based on her lies, I decided I was going to write them a letter explaining the true story. I have decided to share this letter with you. It is word for word what I sent to the diocese tribunal. (I have deleted names and used generic terms for certain people because no need to drag other people into this with the whole world, I even replaced my ex wife's name with words like she, her, my ex wife, etc. I don't want her to have another excuse to try and extort money from me.)

This is the letter I sent them:

November 26, 2008

To: _____ Diocese

From: Todd Thiede

Re: Marriage annulment

To whom it may concern:

I am writing this letter in response to my wife seeking an annulment of our marriage. I am sorry to say but I am not looking for this annulment to go through. I don't feel everything was done to save this marriage by my ex wife. Not only this but as I look for a definition of annulment I find this:

"An annulment, properly called a decree of nullity, is a finding by a church tribunal that ON THE DAY VOWS WERE EXCHANGED at least some essential element for a valid marriage was lacking. An annulment does not concern whether a marriage was a happy one, whether one

of the spouses LATER became unfaithful (which I did not do and she did), or LATER decided to not have children (which we did have a beautiful daughter during our marriage)but only their intention on the wedding day!! If a marriage was made on that day it is a life long bond, irrespective of what happened later in that marriage.

Now my ex wife is going to say she did everything in her power to save this marriage. That statement is totally 100% false. She just presented a letter to me requesting release of information from my personal therapist about our marriage. Unfortunately this therapist was not a marriage counselor for us. She was my kids counselor and after I was told by my wife that she wanted a divorce she was my personal counselor. Let me explain. On October 31, 2005 we were at my brother and sister-in-laws home for trick or treating with the kids. My wife and I were talking about having another baby. (NOTHING OUT OF THE ORDINARY ABOUT THAT. WE EVEN DISCUSSED NAMES.) I remember this very well because it was only 2 weeks later that my wife dropped the bomb on me about not wanting to be married anymore by stating (and I quote) "I don't want to be married anymore...not just to you, I don't want to be married to anyone at all...I would much rather live with my parents...I had more fun with them" (Yep only 2 weeks after wanting another child together) It was at this time I slid into a deep depression (I don't want to meet any person that doesn't get depressed when the person you wanted to spend your whole life with tells you that they don't want the same)and sought help understanding myself and getting myself right with what has just happened. Although my wife did come with me to see my therapist one time it was not to discuss our marriage it was to discuss me. She refused to discuss our marriage at this session. However, I did try to set up counseling sessions with Father _____ (I deleted his name because it is not his fault he really did try) of the church we were married in. She refused to go to these sessions and even told Father the reason for not going is "because she didn't want to hear how marriage is forever and that she didn't want to hear how she should try and make a marriage work, because she just didn't want to make it work, she didn't want to be married anymore!!" I however did keep appointments with Father and told him all that was going on in my life. I even tried talking with my wife's own parents. Her father being a deacon at this church I thought could help me convince my wife of her vows of marriage before God and the church and help her go into counseling with Father . However, her father stated that he can't give me any advice and he will not talk to his daughter about this because she has made up her mind and she doesn't want to be married anymore. 2 months after my wife moved in with her parents I was able to blackmail her into going to see a marriage counselor. Yes I admit openly I used blackmail to get her to go. I firmly believed in this marriage and I was using anything and everything to try and save it just like I believe God would have wanted. The way I got her into this counseling was to state that I would grant her a divorce if she went. Prior to this I told her I would never grant her a divorce. The counselor we saw that evening was not my personal therapist. It was a counselor referred to me by a person I work with that helped her parents out when they went through a very tough time in their marriage. I will be happy to release any information obtained by this counselor. But I am sure that my ex wife will not want that information to be released because it would show the counsel the truth and not the lies she is trying to get you to believe. But I will not release private information from my personal therapist about my kids counseling or my own personal counseling. I can summarize this counseling session by the last statement the marriage counselor made to me and I am paraphrasing here. There is nothing that I can do when one person (my ex wife) doesn't live up to her vows of marriage and does not want to attempt to save her marriage.

I remember going through 4 weeks of premarital classes for the privilege of getting married in the Catholic church, which both my wife and I did together. I was happy to go through it and so was she, which tells me she was ready to get married and wanted to get married. It is shocking that to get married in the Catholic church you have to go through premarital classes but to get a divorce or annulment from the Catholic church there is no class you have to go through to try and save a marriage first. No required reading, no required counseling, absolutely nothing!!

I firmly believe that if you speak to Father and the marriage counselor you will see nothing was done to prevent this divorce from happening by my wife.

My wife, born and raised Catholic doesn't respect the sanctity of marriage as she should. The man she was dating before we met (Bill was his name). Was not only 20 years older than her but was still married at the time they were together and while we were married she had developed a personal relationship with a married father of one of the boys on my sons football team.

Even though she had developed this relationship with this man, I was and am willing to save our marriage, even though my wife refused to seek any kind of help for our marriage. I WAS AND I AM STILL WILLING SEEK HELP TO SAVE IT!! I did everything I possibly could do to save this marriage and I am still willing to save the marriage that was sworn before God in November 2002. Even though the state of Illinois and the County of Dupage say that we are divorced, we are still married in the eyes of the church and The Eyes of our Lord and Savior because I swore before him and witnesses on that day to be married to her until death do us part.

It is for these reasons that an annulment should not be granted. This marriage should be upheld by the Catholic Church.

If you have any further questions feel free to contact me again at (847) ***-**** or you can contact me via U.S. mail at the address you sent your request to.

Thank you for your time.

Todd Thiede

Like I said that was the exact letter I sent to the diocese office (I had it saved in my computer) in response to my ex wife's request for an annulment. The only thing I did was take out some names to protect their privacy. Do you realize that it only took 2 weeks for the diocese to answer my letter and you will probably guess what they had to say. (I am paraphrasing here because I was so frustrated that I shredded the letter)

The letter started out thanking me for responding to their questionnaire and they wanted to commend me for wanting to work out my marriage with my ex wife. They said even if an annulment were granted that doesn't mean the marriage is completely over. They have seen many people go through an annulment procedure and still reconcile their relationship and get married to each other again. They then proceeded to thank me again for responding and said if I have any further questions to contact them.

What did that sound like to you? To me it sounded like a complete and utter blow off!! They didn't care about facts (I checked with the marriage counselor. They never contacted her in any way shape or form), they didn't care about what is right or wrong. They didn't care about true Catholic Church procedure. They didn't care about anything except the money. See to get an annulment you have to pay the church tribunal a fee. And because I am not the one that requested the annulment and I am not the one that paid the fee they didn't care about what I had to say or for that matter what the true facts were. The fee 6 years ago when I went for the annulment of my first marriage was 500 dollars, so I am assuming that fee went up. So because my ex wife bribed the church the right amount of money she gets what she wants. I wonder if I offered them more money if they would turn down her annulment request.

Had I known then what I know now I would have never ever gotten my first marriage annulled. The Catholic Church annulled that marriage no problem. Based on what I have read recently when doing research for this book I believe they should not have annulled my first marriage. I firmly believe this because at the time my first wife and I were married we met all the rules I stated earlier for a marriage to be a true marriage in the eyes of the church. Our intentions at that time was to have it last forever. Granted it did not work out that way but again had I known then what I know now about what an annulment means and what it requires I would not have been able to do it with a true conscience. I may be an asshole but I am not a lying one. I want what is right and just and I know now that I should have never been granted that first annulment.

So what does this all mean? It means if you pay the fees/bribes to the church you can do whatever you want and they won't care because they got their money. They only care about what you can do for them. The Catholic Church (any organized church or religion for that matter) only cares about the almighty dollar not about the true all mighty God. You can break sacrament after sacrament and it is OK because all you have to do is buy your way out of it. Commit a sin back in the day it would require you to say hail Mary's as penance now it is say hail Mary's and 50 bucks too (or more). If you give them enough money you don't have to worry about right and wrong in the church.

Organized Religion is truly MESSED UP!!

CONCLUSION

In conclusion I would like to say "is this country perfect?" No!! However, I will say this again this is the best country on this entire planet. All we need to do now is tweak it just a little bit and we can not only rebound from our current economic situation but we can correct a lot of problems that I brought to your attention in this book. If we as a people want to change it we can. That is the beauty of this country and its democracy. If we don't like something we vote in someone else who's policies we do like and hopefully that helps. If not, we do it all over again. These problem areas I talked about in this book can be fixed and fixing them will strengthen our country like never before. All we have to do as a country is start worrying about our country only. That means all of our countrymen. We will not pick and choose who to stand behind because we are all created equal and we are all in this together!! As for the other countries in this world SCREW EM!!!

If you have any questions or comments and want to contact me directly you can at toddthiede@aol.com (yep I am an American through and through I even use the ISP named after our country) I truly look forward

Todd M. Thiede

to hearing from you all. Take care, God bless, and good
luck to us all!!